Experiences of Person-Centred Counselling Training

by
Laura Buchanan
and Rick Hughes

PCCS BOOKS
Ross-on-Wye

First published in 2000

PCCS BOOKS Ltd
Llangarron
Ross-on-Wye
Herefordshire
HR9 6PT
UK
Tel +44 (0)1989 77 07 07

Experiences of Person-centred Counselling Training

ISBN 1 898059 15 2

Cover design by Denis Postle.
Printed by Redwood Books, Trowbridge, Wiltshire, UK

person-centred counselling training

contents

contents

dedica-tions

Laura Buchanan
To Buck.

Rick Hughes
To Linn Clark, who opened my eyes to a new way of being.

please note

fore-
word

In my study I have a letter from Carl Rogers, dated January 4, 1987 — exactly a month before his death aged 85 years. Within the letter he writes:

> *'I am excited about the idea of a book which focuses on the client's experience of the counselling process. In our "client-centered approach" we start from the experiencing of our client, but seldom do we give that experience center stage in our academic writing'.*

Even at 85 years of age Carl was passionate about grounding our learning on the client's perspective. I am sure he would, similarly, have found it exciting to read this book produced entirely by recent person-centred counselling trainees and comprising the experience of their peers. There are precious few texts explicitly about person-centred counselling training and those which are written by trainers must be regarded with the appropriate suspicion that they may be offering a gloss on events.

This book is written for trainees, therefore it must be read by trainers. Nor should they feel apprehensive about the prospect, for the critique offered by their former trainees is both balanced and considerate as well as insightful. Also, many parts of the book cover areas where the trainer has no direct experience, such as the moving section on the impact of the training experience upon relations with peers, partners and parents.

Equally engrossing is the very first section, 'How and why I got into counselling'. This contained such a variety and intensity of human experience that it demands attention from us trainers. We are receiving into our care a wide selection of human beings whose life experiences have led them to believe that it is important that they seek to make a difference. This section reminded me of a counsellor I met in Liverpool. No-one would ever have predicted that his early working life on the factory floor would be followed by a career in counselling — but then, nobody would have predicted Hillsborough.

Some counselling trainers might be apprehensive about this book — it is possible that it may deter some prospective trainees. My own view is that, hopefully, this will be the case.

Dave Mearns
University of Strathclyde, Counselling Dept.
Glasgow
April 2000

experiences of

person-centred counselling training

preface

BAC: The British Association for Counselling. Publishes a journal (*Counselling*) ten times a year. It produces several other publications of interest to counsellors, clients and the general public on counselling-related topics including the *Counselling and Psychotherapy Resources Directory*, listing counsellors, supervisors and training organisations in the UK.

How and why this book was developed

This book has been developed in response to a plea from people who have gone through counselling training. But it is aimed at people who may be about to embark on training. Former trainees frequently mentioned to us that they were blissfully unaware of the degree of work, commitment and energy which would be required for their respective training. We asked whether they would have liked to have had some sort of insight before hand. Their answer was universally, 'yes'. Subsequently, their support, cajoling and enthusiasm, prompted us to plan a book which met this need.

Initially we conducted a pilot research exercise to determine what style and format the book should take. It seemed a case study review would be of most interest, providing an opportunity to canvas former trainees throughout the UK, on a wide range of types of person-centred courses. We started off with an advertisement in the November 1997 issue of Counselling Journal, wherein we invited potential contributors to make contact with us. Initially some fifty people responded, asking for further information. We sent by return what we referred to as the 'Contributor's Information Pack'. This explained what the book was about and how we sought contributions from former trainees, people who had experience of counselling training. We added to this sample a mailing to the course director of every person-centred training institution in the UK, as identified by the 1996 BAC Counselling & Psychotherapy Resource Directory.

The 'Contributor's Information Pack' listed some sixty topic areas which we had identified as being significant to the training experience. During a ten month period, we received a steady flow of case study contributions. We invited our potential contributors to write as much or as little as they wanted on any or all of the sixty topic areas. Significantly, over ninety per cent of responses related to just twenty seven topic areas - less than fifty per cent of the original list.

To present a manageable and representative range of case studies, we reduced this down to twenty five chapters and these are the ones represented in the book. In this way, we feel we can claim to be 'contributor-centred'! We wish to convey our thanks to the contributors who we've been able to acknowledge by name and the many more who either sent in anonymous material or wished not to be mentioned.

We acknowledged that the format of this book does suffer from several limitations. In several chapters, the case study material may be biased towards one view, rather than another. This should not reflect the reality of an overall perspective and we have tried to highlight this when this has come to our notice. Having said this, we felt it important to be receptive to the views of the contributors. Whether it is representative in the statistical sense, it is impossible to say.

One concern raised during the development of the text was that we might be guilty of feeding biased thoughts and expectations into the minds of potential counselling recruits. We acknowledge there is this potential and state that this is not our intention. This is a compendium of testimonies — experiences which chart the training and development of counselling trainees. In some sense, as we break into the new millennium, this represents the development of training of the person-centred approach in Britain during the 1990's. A comparison some ten years hence would make excellent reading.

This book is not a step-by-step guide intended to give the reader all the answers to the many questions that applicants to counselling training might have. In fact, we hope we provoke many more questions than answers. The purpose here is to offer an insight into training. Readers who are already in training can reflect on the similarities and differences of situations and comments. Seasoned counsellors and other former trainees may find the book useful as they reflect on their experiences. Whoever you are, at whatever stage you are, this book is written for people interested in counselling, by people interested in counselling.

How this book should be read
Our first point is that there is no *best* way this book should be read. Over 250 case-studies are featured covering 25 subject areas, some of which will be of interest to you more than others. The format has been devised so you can dip in and out at will. Each chapter has a short introduction within which both Laura and Rick add some of their own personal experiences. The introductions set the scene and offer a way into the case-studies.

The case-studies are taken from a total sample of those submitted and we have triedto ensure that they do represent a reasonably realistic account of what is happening out there in the world of person-centred counselling training. Some chapters have more contributions than others and again this is representative of the total proportion of the submitted entries.

To protect anonymity, names and places have been changed. All names which introduce a case-study are similarly fictitious. We have not altered the tone, manner and style, only the readability. After the selection of case-studies, we have summarised each chapter with a section entitled *Points to Ponder*, encouraging you, the reader, to do just that!

We hope you enjoy this book and that this helps support your interest in counselling.

Rick Hughes and Laura Buchanan — April 2000

experiences of

person-centred counselling training

acknowledgements

This book has taken several years to develop. It would not have been possible but for the help, support and advice provided by a number of people, including James Withey, an inspirational member of the initial editorial team whose enthusiasm, humour and contribution leaves a lasting mark. We were sorry that his illness meant he was unable to commit further. Also to Pete Sanders & Maggie Taylor-Sanders at PCCS Books, for their belief in and commitment to us as well as their endeavours to advance Person-centred counselling. We'd also like to thank Professor Dave Mearns, Heather Robertson and Norma Craig at the Counselling Unit, University of Strathclyde. A special thank you goes to Graeme Buchanan, who helped us keep in touch across several continents.

And of course to the universities, colleges and training centres who enabled us to get in touch with their current and former trainees. But the biggest thank you goes out to all those who submitted material to us. These individuals invested time, effort and thought offering us an insight into their experiences, sometimes traumatic, often very personal but ultimately helping us to provide an insight into the experience of person-centred counselling training in the UK.

A large number of contributors asked us not to include their names or submitted material anonymously. This suggested to us how the journey of counselling training can be a very private experience and a difficult one to share with readers who are not known to the contributors.

We also thank the other contributors who, with their permission, we're happy to acknowledge by name. Thank you Annette Ansell, Jane Balmforth, Julia Bird, Vada Brain, Christine Brown, Bruce Corr, Christine Couldridge, Dani Dale, Caroline Hattersley, Christina Karagianni, Isie MacIntyre, Abdullah Popoola, Peter Roberts, Wanda Tebby, Keith Trivasse and David Woodall.

Laura would like to conclude with — I would like to say thank you to my co-author and friend Rick Hughes. Rick's commitment and professionalism throughout our project has been an essential part of the process of writing this book. His drive, organisation and humour are fundamental to his way of working and I feel privileged that we've been able to work together.

And Rick — Thank you to Laura who has been able to commit, support and contribute fully to the two-person editing process even whilst living abroad. Her calmness and sense of perspective has not only been a key mediating influence on the project but has reminded me of the value and significance of true friendships.

section a

how and why I got into counsel- ling training

If a child is asked what they want to be when they grow up, they may suggest a fire-fighter, a nurse, a dancer or a soldier but probably not a counsellor. This is not to say that counselling is unfashionable or unknown — it is growing and developing at breakneck speeds, and it still has huge unrealised potential.

Counselling is a job that people *develop into*. So what is counselling and how do we define it? The problem with a definition is that it can be constricting and restricting. Furthermore, there are several mainstream styles or approaches of counselling and each will operate slightly differently. This book concentrates on the Person-Centred Approach, the format which is probably most used today in the UK. Rather than to attempt to define person-centred counselling, it is hoped the meaning held by the various contributors will evolve for you by the end of this book.

Counselling cannot be learnt just from textbooks. Trainees need to understand how this *works* — it is known as the *process* of counselling. This involves the development of a therapeutic relationship between a client and a counsellor. A trainee needs to have a good knowledge of themselves — sometimes known as *self-awareness*. This self-awareness helps to manage personal issues which might otherwise get in the way of a counselling or therapeutic relationship. For example, a counsellor who has a mother with cancer may find it very difficult to work with a client who has cancer — the personal connection may *infect* the client/counsellor work.

Self-awareness is a key ingredient of person-centred counselling and links with personal traits or parts of our personality and affects our values, beliefs, attitudes, perceptions etc. In fact, many people may consider counselling training *because of* something that happens in their life causing them to review or to change their values and beliefs — what they find important to them, how they value themselves and others. Several case-studies mention changing attitudes which prompted consideration of counselling training, in some cases this was initiated by internal factors — how they started to see things differently, or by external factors — how work forced them to review their options.

This Section covers how people have *moved towards* becoming a counsellor — what were their motivations? What appears to be consistent from the case-studies is the value and importance attached to getting professional training. This could well be a biased view because case-study contributions were, in the main, sought from training institutions, so it is possible that such a view should be expected. However, there are a large number of people who claim to be

At the time of writing, the British Association for Counselling has approximately 17,000 members (of which around 3000 are 'Accredited'). This covers counsellors practising in a variety of therapeutic approaches, not just the Person-Centred Approach. This figure, however, does not include the many counsellors who are not members of BAC and/or who are members of other associations.

BAC: British Association for Counselling.
COSCA: Confederation of Scottish Counselling Agencies.
Both publish Codes of Ethics and Practice which members agree to abide by.

If you want further information about BAC:
Tel: 01788 578 328
email: bac@co.uk
www.counselling.co.uk
BAC
1 Regent Place
Rugby
Warwickshire
CV21 2PJ

If you want further information about COSCA:
Tel: 01786 475 140
COSCA 18 Viewfield St
Stirling
SK8 1UA
Scotland

The Independent Practitioners' Network and Association of Humanistic Psychology Practitioners also produce codes of ethics which bind members. Contact details for these organisations can be found in Appendix 3.

You may wish to check out a number of organisations to find out which ones best suit your needs.

counsellors, with or without professional training, and, while there is no statutory regulation to insist on a basic standard of training, some professional counselling associations require members to abide by a Code of Ethics, for example, BAC and COSCA. Their Codes map out the responsibilities and professionalism expected of counsellors when working with their clients. At the time of writing, there is limited sanction for those counsellors who stray from what is deemed acceptable behaviour or practice. If a counsellor is a member of a professional counselling association, they will be bound by the appropriate Code of Ethics as a condition of membership. However, membership is not a quality guarantee. If someone was to fall foul of the Code, disciplinary proceedings may be evoked by the professional body. They may then conclude with recommendations for re-training or other corrective action or exclusion from the professional body in question, but at the end of the day, with no legal requirement to be a member of a professional association, an individual would be able to continue practice, albeit without the membership of that association.

There has recently been increasing speculation regarding statutory regulation of counselling and psychotherapy. This would mean some form of legal training requirement, such as exists for solicitors or medical doctors. As this looms closer, people who want to become counsellors understand the need for professional training. It is likely that employers will increasingly only want counsellors who have had a recognised training. Quite apart from this, counsellors have a basic moral and ethical responsibility to the public and our clients to provide a safe and professional service. Recent media stories have highlighted alleged unscrupulous practitioners and, when accurate, do help deter those who should not be practising. Such stories, however, also damage the reputation and fine work of the vast majority of counsellors. Training is a basic prerequisite and it exists to give us the skills, knowledge and values to be effective counsellors. Although necessary, training to be a counsellor is by no means easy, as the rest of this book will demonstrate. If training to be a counsellor turns out to be the right thing for you, it is likely to be one of the most challenging, rewarding, emotive, intimate and dramatic experiences in your life.

Section A looks at why and how people decided to commit to counselling training, what jobs they were doing before and what their motivations were. You will notice in Chapter 1 that people have had some very varied jobs and shows there is no hard and fast rule as to the 'best' route into counselling.

Chapter 2 asks about the motivation to help others, specifically whether this enthusiasm is based on a *need* to help or a *want* to help. If we *need* to help, what is this saying about us? Does this need meet some unfulfilled aspect of our lives and if so what sort of impact would this have on our clients? For example, if someone were to lose their role as a carer — the children grow up and leave home, or an elderly parent dies — there may still be a remaining 'need' to continue to help and a feeling of loss of that person. This 'gap' might then be filled by counselling training. So we would be entering into training because of an unfulfilled, and possibly unexplored, need rather than an authentic feeling of wanting to help someone.

Chapter 3 explores why and how people chose not just counselling training but one which follows the Person-Centred Approach. There are many counselling approaches, and there are many other forms of personal help, including the work of psychologists, psychiatrists, psychotherapists, hypnotherapists etc. The focus for this book is the person-centred counselling approach. If a reader wished to evaluate other counselling approaches, and other helping professions, they would be advised to consult with books which specifically refer to these subjects and where much more appropriate depth can be found. Appendix 2 provides a brief list of further recommended reading.

**experi-
ences
of**

**person-centred
counselling
training**

1
what was I doing before?

In this chapter we will look at the previous professions and jobs of former trainees. In what areas of work or study were they involved? Is there a link between this and their current training? Do trainees feel that their previous experience can assist or enhance any aspect of their new counselling career? What encouraged and stimulated these individuals to move on and train in counselling? Many people change career or take a sideroad off the main path of their profession, but it's interesting to consider why some people choose counselling. Perhaps by understanding someone else's motivation, it may offer you further insight into your own reason for embarking on this journey.

In the following case-studies you will see a wide range of previous occupations in which people were involved, ranging through secretarial, youth and community work, teaching, management, engineering, research, advertising to nursing. Each person has come to counselling through their own route. Laura's own process evolved from the helping professions. She recognised that she needed further training in working with people. The primary reason for this was to help her work at greater depth in a 'safe' way for the client and herself. In this context, 'safe' refers to the responsibility we have towards our clients to ensure the appropriateness of support that we offer which is not potentially damaging for a client.

It is amazing to think that you are able to use disparate bits and pieces of knowledge and experience in a new career, to start to recognise that everything with which you have been involved could be useful. But that's the way it is in counselling, a huge pot of soup with different flavours blending together to create something new. All of our experiences, emotions and ideas are valid and offer a rich cauldron from which to draw. You may be able to tap into a past personal experience to allow you to empathise with how a client feels. Although you will be experiencing the client's world through their descriptions and senses, it may help you feel more connected by understanding the worth of all the work with which you have been involved.

Some people feel that the 'right' route is through the other 'helping professions' and then on to postgraduate training in counselling. However, although this is a fairly common route it is by no means the only one. You may have worked in a bakery, office or abattoir . . . so might your client! (A client who is coming to a counsellor wants to meet a *real* person, so a mixture of experiences helps to balance out the relationship between you and your client.)

We hope that you will be able to see that there is no right or wrong route into counselling. As the case-studies demonstrate, this is a profession that attracts people from all walks of life. The varied backgrounds of counsellors offer the profession and the client a rich pool of experience and uniqueness that would be lost if we all hailed from the same source.

The case-studies also touch on the motivation for training as a counsellor. There are two common themes running through the case-studies:
1. the trainee feels the need to change their life; and
2. a feeling that something is missing from their current area of work.

From this we noticed a consistent theme where respondents were addressing the need to correct a lack of involvement with people. Others were directly working with people but wished to enhance their abilities to equip them for developing deeper and more real relationships. For some trainees it is the result of personal experiences that initiates an interest in counselling.

Rick's path into counselling was a mix of the above. He worked in business and both wanted to make a change and felt something was missing. It was his desire to work with people at a deeper level that prompted him into considering counselling as a career.

We have not heard from anyone who chose to enter the counselling profession straight from school or pre-university. There is some debate in the profession regarding the minimum age requirement set by some counselling courses. We imagine that individuals who demonstrate at an early age their desire to work in the 'caring professions', are probably diverted into areas such as nursing, medicine, occupational therapy and psychology rather than counselling.

The case-studies are real-life quotations, featured just as we received them. They allow for your own personal interpretation. However, we have left you with some summary comments at the end of the chapter, featured under *Points to Ponder*.

In both the US and the UK there is a history of young people learning counselling to help each other. This usually happens through a voluntary agency or school or students' union and is called *peer counselling*. There is nothing in person-centred theory or practice that strongly suggests that anyone can be too young to offer the core conditions.

Charlene   In my short working life I have worked in many different areas: retail management, finance, the law; I have done secretarial work, residential youth work, community-based youth work and various aspects of pastoral work. All of these have in many ways shaped my current career as a counsellor and therapist.

Beforehand I was a mother and housewife until my marriage deteriorated in 1993.   **Imelda**
I then started a Sociology course with the Open University and graduated two years ago. Prior to having my children I was a secretary for a Personnel Director.

Clare   I have had a very varied career, lived for many years in both Holland and Malaysia. I returned to Britain in 1988 and joined a weight-loss company as a centre manager. My work involved not only the financial responsibility and running of the centre but offering a form of counselling and teaching to clients. In 1989 I met my husband to be. A year later he admitted himself to the local psychiatric hospital to address his addiction to alcohol. I joined Al-Anon, a self-help group for the family and friends of problem drinkers. Al-Anon helped me come to terms with my own emotional distress and allowed me to uncover the harmful emotional effects of the sexual abuse in my childhood. I sought personal counselling realising that, as helpful as Al-Anon had been, I needed more help than was on offer. Over the following years I became disillusioned with the help I was offering clients at work and set up on my own. As I worked with my private weight-loss clients, deep issues began to arise for them and I realised I needed formal counselling training if I were to remain of ethical help. That was when I began my training.

Charlotte

Prior to beginning my counselling training course I was working in project management within the pharmaceutical industry. I had taken a Science degree aged 18–22 and at the age of 31 decided I no longer wanted to continue with a career within a scientific arena. The lack of involvement with people was the main factor in my dissatisfaction.

Dwight

Two years before I started training I had been made redundant from a large multinational engineering company. Two years before this I had been able to satisfy my social belief of contributing on a voluntary basis, time and some skills I had, to the community.

Miranda

My root to counselling training is rather roundabout. After a degree in English I taught English as a foreign language in Budapest for three years and then in Paris for five years. While in Paris I joined The Samaritans and the training had a profound effect on me, changing the way I listened to people and responded to them. Although at this time I was rather full of what I saw as my 'lady bountiful' role, this was the start of the path that took me to counselling training. When I left Paris in 1990 I tried unsuccessfully to be accepted onto a social work course and worked for The Samaritans and Victim Support in the UK before joining Voluntary Services Overseas (VSO) and going to the Philippines to teach English. I then got a job as a VSO staff member in the Field Office in Manila and among my many tasks one was supporting the volunteers who came out to projects in the Philippines. The issues that volunteers encountered, both personal and professional, would fill a book! I enjoyed dealing with issues which ranged from unwanted and wanted pregnancies, harassment, serious illness, evacuation from a project, relationship problems, work problems, homesickness . . . it was a thorough training in the human condition and revived in me thoughts of doing a qualification in something 'caring', thoughts which had been rather dashed after my non-acceptance for the CQSW for which I had absolutely no background at all!

Anne

I had been working in a voluntary project doing research and education and had developed another project as a result of my research. The committee of the original project wanted to separate the two organisations with which I was attached, including having two committees. I was to return to the original project, when I had finished the second one, on the original mission. During this work I had developed considerably, both as a person and with the skills I had. But I could not face going back to what I perceived as fairly non-dynamic work. During this time my research committee disbanded, ultimately making me redundant. I was unemployed for four months before finding another job.

Rob

My background was really diverse. After a fairly abysmal clutch of 'A' levels I managed to get into university where I read Commerce. I really enjoyed this and, as well as gaining a 2.1, managed to build into this a Marketing placement at a car manufacturer. Thereafter I worked for an event management company, contemplated self-employment and then settled into Advertising. I then met a woman who changed my life forever. If I was a born-again Capitalist, she was a born-again Socialist! Our opposites attracted and we began to merge to a common ground. But I was also getting progressively unsettled in advertising; my company was paying me a pittance whilst I was slogging my guts out. I was losing motivation for this profession. My partner came along and helped me open a door to a new way of being, a new approach and a new set of values. What freaked me out during all this was the realisation that I pretty well had zilch values anyway, in fact I didn't really know who I was or what I wanted. I had had dreams of running my own advertising agency one day and believed I had a mentor who was grooming me for this — the realities were quite different. I still had great enthusiasm and energy but nowhere where this could be realised.

Lavinia

I previously worked as an occupational therapist. I specialised in working with clients with mental health problems. The most rewarding, and frustrating, aspect of my job involved the process of 'getting to know the client'. At times this could be very stimulating and exhilarating and I would be left with the feeling that I was really getting somewhere. At other times it could be a most frustrating and protracted situation. In retrospect I recognise that this was related to boundaries, i.e. how we build protective mechanisms. I worked to a defined code of ethics, designed by the British Association of Occupational Therapists. But there is something else which we need to understand, that is our philosophy and where this stems from.

I feel, now, that the issue was about understanding my personal boundaries. During counselling training I explored many half-hidden areas which helped me to understand my feelings and responses to particular situations. As a result I can now, most of the time, recognise if personal material is being triggered or touched in me by a client's story. On some occasions I realised that my clouded understanding of my own responses and attitudes to a client was limiting the connection and relationship with them. At times, I was feeling unsafe and unclear of my boundaries with the client.

points to ponder

- There is no *best way* into counselling. Many people do come from other 'helping' or 'caring' professions but this does not mean that they are more suitable than those who do not.

- Equally, age offers no benchmark for suitability for training as a counsellor. Noone can say that it is 'better' to be aged 49 than 29. Perhaps the criteria for suitability needs to focus more on *maturity* and *competence* factors which are not necessarily tied to specific age ranges.

- You may find that your past experience can both help and hinder your training efforts. On the one hand, each of us can take our past and current experiences into new situations believing that they will be automatically applicable to the new situation, when in reality, they are not. For example, a lack of awareness or prejudices to particular problems may impact on your client work and interaction with fellow colleagues. On the other hand, you may be able to draw on past experience (personal or work related) to help you understand and develop within your training course. Presumably your past experience will have helped shape your decision to train as a counsellor.

- Part of moving *into* counselling training can be moving *away* from a previous job. You may experience a period of transition especially at the beginning of training when everything seems very new and unfamiliar. You may feel uncomfortable and challenged by the new approach offered by your training course. You may feel stimulated and elated by the new material and situations to which you are exposed. You may experience a synthesis between your past work and training experience and your current training course. Or you may experience a range of contradictory feelings as you try to retain a degree of balance. Remember, however, a training course should be an ideal environment to explore these feelings and their changing nature.

- A common theme running through the case-studies is a feeling of dissatisfaction with former work situations. This resulted in many of the individuals changing or redefining their occupation. One of their ways of changing was to 'test the water' of counselling training. For instance, Rob talks of his move away from a product-focused commercial area of work to the desire to work with people. However, later, Rob may find his experience in commerce and marketing invaluable — each of us has valuable and unique experiences to bring to counselling training.

- The case-studies give us a hint as to how and why some people eventually chose to pursue counselling training, for example, Dwight had been made redundant and Anne's situation was not dissimilar. However, Clare became closely involved in counselling as a result of her connection with Al-Anon.

**2
do you
want to
help or do
you *need*
to help?**

'Do you *want* to help or do you *need* to help?' This is an interesting question and is one which cannot be answered with a simple 'yes' or 'no'. The Oxford English Dictionary identifies *want* as 'require, need' and *need* as 'stand in need of, require, be under necessity or obligation to or to do', so there are clearly overlaps between the two words in standard English. However, the distinction in the language of counselling is illustrated by the perception of the meaning of *need*, highlighting feelings of obligation and necessity. This suggests an imbalance in the relationship when a need is being served rather than a 'want'.

Needing to help suggests that the need is coming from the individual and that the individual has no control over this feeling. A client exposed to this may lose their sense of their own power within the relationship and hand over responsibility for their personal choice to the counsellor. *Wanting* to help suggests that the counsellor is offering an opportunity to develop a therapeutic relationship on the *client's own* terms. The client who experiences *this* may then feel that they have the right to say 'no'.

The emphasis in person-centred counselling is on the client and counsellor developing a relationship based on equality, openness and acceptance. If this can exist in the counselling relationship, it creates a safe environment in which the client may explore the issues causing them concern. It can alert both client and counsellor to times when the relationship might be moving away from a safe environment, when, perhaps, raw issues suddenly become apparent and openness can also allow for the opportunity to choose how and whether a client wants to explore a specific avenue or not.

Something that jumps out from each case-study is that helping others comes from *feeling* rather than a studied or conscious choice. There is a sense of this desire or feeling going through some process of evolution or development. Part of your training may be starting to understand the evolution of your needs and wants in relation to helping. In this way you may be able to recognise the areas and issues in your life which may trigger in you the 'needing to help' or the 'wanting to help'.

It can, however, be difficult to clarify the issue of needing or wanting to help — it may not be simply and neatly dealt with once and put in the 'out-tray'. A trainee may discover that he/she is responding to a specific client in a way which is different from their usual relationship with other clients or may feel perplexed as to why there is a feeling of a 'need to help' with one client and not another.

Laura worked with a client where she became conscious of needing to help. This became apparent through Laura's desire to protect the client and hurry her to a conclusion in her counselling process. Obviously this didn't work, but the process between the therapist and client changed when Laura shared her current feelings and internal reactions with the client in question. The client triggered in Laura her need to protect people who are being treated unfairly, rather than helping the person to learn to deal with the situation independently.

The potential effects of any one relationship are boundless. Both parties are bringing with them their unique experiences and sense of life, in a cocktail which doesn't have a recipe. The trainee counsellor will not be able to anticipate which client may trigger strong feelings. If the trainee has an awareness of their feelings, it will help their understanding of what is happening in the relationship. This is an ongoing process not just for the trainee counsellor but for all of us working with individuals in a therapeutic way.

Each of the case-studies offers different and personal interpretations of needing and wanting to help. There also appears to be a transition from needing to help to wanting to help, fuelled by the trainee's increasing self-awareness. With each client and significant presenting issue, you may notice different emotions and responses springing from you. Need and want are not negative and positive, rather they are emotions which may provoke quite different actions and reactions in you towards your client. These can be powerful feelings and it may be enough to simply acknowledge this rather than to label them as either negative or positive.

Rick is reminded of an interview he attended for a counselling post. One particular question jarred with him then, 'Do you love your clients?'. To him this seemed a strange question but it did make him think. He felt he was being asked about his motivation to help — where did this come from? His answer was that as a person he really valued and respected people and this parallels with his work with clients. As a result of his own counselling training he still clings to what may seem an idealistic ambition, that of contributing to making the world a more contented place. He may not always be successful in this endeavour but his motivation, enthusiasm and interest in people is what drives him.

Charlotte   I believe my need to help has been partly instinctual and partly instilled by my Christian upbringing. From my schooldays, I was involved in helping activities, finding my identity through responding to the needs of myself and others. Being the first-born daughter, with a sister ten years younger, I voluntarily adopted a mothering role for many years and as I was growing older I offered a lot of time and attention to other people in listening and trying to support their needs. Struggling with my adolescence and the strained relations in my family as well as my need to set limits upon my responses to the requirements of others, I was left with a persistent wish to understand human nature and to use my understanding in helping people, including myself, overcome life difficulties and live more effectively.

Ken

I knew, but could not (would not) say, how much pure pleasure I got out of being able to positively help people. And how much worth, real, tangible worth I got from this. And I knew just whom I was pleasing, and why, and how. Yet there was a different worth also involved, not mere propitiation of a god who would consume unless appeased but also the worth of finding some kind of meaning in a process. I found some kind of meaning for me and I knew that others found meaning through the process; it was the fear of meaninglessness that counselling helped ward off.

Charlie

I feel my 'need' to help others stems from two sources. I have a desire to make 'whole', which I believe comes from feeling fragmented myself for so much of my life. And the belief that when a person understands his/her self, self-determination and understanding of others can be achieved; that as a species we can 'join' and solve many (if not all) of our common problems. I am of course aware of the grandioseness of this concept, however, it remains a personal motivation.

Jules

My *need to help* goes back a long way and is something that I have had to work on in PPD Groups [Personal and Professional Development Groups during counselling training] on the course and also in personal therapy. As the oldest of six sisters I was brought up with a strong helping ethic, that not to help was bad. Since then I have often taken responsibility to help and be the one to put things right even when it is not expected of me. I have now achieved a greater awareness of what this need is and, though I still get the urge with clients to make it OK for them, I am better able to control it. There is still a lot to be done in this area though!

Angie

It was how I learned that my strongest impulse was to rescue, thereby not allowing someone in difficulties the satisfaction of having worked out the problem for themselves.

Roger

This was a fascinating point to consider but it came to me once in training rather than beforehand. I wanted to help people because I had what seemed to be an innate sense of sharing and togetherness, so *support* was also in there somewhere. I valued people and I liked people. Everytime I churned out a CV, it would have my 'liking people' bit splashed all over it. But even though I liked people, it wasn't until my training that I considered how I actually related to people. When I considered whether I *needed* to help, I was shocked to find that this was probably at the heart of my motivation and in what now seems a rather pathetic motivation. I had been going out with this girl called Lori, who was a nurse, and while I was not at that time working in the helping profession, I aspired to her sort of work. She then left me, and the gap or void which I had to contend with was filled with a need to try and win her back. I think I must have felt this would do the trick. Also I think that I was probably in need and I could lose this by feeling needed by others. In retrospect I cringe at how I started my counselling training, yet due to the significant personal development dimension on the course, I was able to work around and beyond this so that when I had completed training, I had redefined my *need* to help to one where I had a genuine *want* to help.

Martha   I really only properly looked at my motivations for helping once I actually got onto my Certificate Course in Counselling Skills. Maybe that was what the course was partly about, partly skills development but also a degree of personal reflection and development. The answer to this ended up causing me great anxiety. I had been a housewife and mother throughout my life. My husband had been a Church of England vicar and I seemed to happily settle into my role supporting him. Honestly though, I did enjoy this but it was only having the focus of personal awareness that I became aware of the needs, desires and wants in me not only with regards to having my own career or job but also for being separate and an individual in my own right rather than the left arm of somebody. Believing strongly in the church environment within which I had lived my life, I wanted to help under my own steam. It was while reflecting on this 'need' to help that I discovered it was a need to do something for me, to help others for my own self-worth, to be valued for me being me. I learned to use this insight to build up my valuing and appreciating of myself and to believe in my abilities and ethical motivations to help others.

I think that I have always wanted to help others. I'm unsure where this urge   *Linn*
originated. I feel part of it lies in my intense satisfaction in developing relationships with others. So perhaps it followed naturally from this sense. I feel that my desire to help others stems from within me, and I experience a personal gratification in being involved in the process. It starts to become a need to help when I think I 'should' be doing it rather than wanting to help. I feel that this is related to personal boundaries. When I am clear regarding my personal boundaries my actions feel right. I have a clear sense of my actions fitting with my emotions. However, when I am unclear about how I feel, I experience difficulty in connecting with my inner world which can help me in making the right choice for me. It is at times like this that I find myself using language such as *should, must, have to*. This is a dangerous point where my ability to recognise *wanting* and *needing* to help becomes fuzzy. It becomes blurred with others' agenda, stray emotions which I'm unable to pin down and isolate, advice from childhood, and values and attitudes which I absorbed growing up and which are still partially hidden to me.

Sarah   I was in about as commercial a job as you probably get — investment management. I liked what I was doing but for me I was dealing with 'things', commodities, companies and investments — there was no real person identifiable behind these facades and I came to a conclusion that I need more . . . I needed to help. There was a need-deficiency in my life. I needed to be part of something where people were the centre. I wanted to make a difference.

It was with some surprise following this counselling session that I had the clarity   *Paul*
of vision to realise that I needed to embark on full-time counselling training which would then equip me to offer support to teachers, who, like me, were experiencing difficulties concerning aspects of their careers and pressures attributed to the speed of change in the profession.

• Do you want to help or do you need to help? Can you see a distinction between wanting and needing to help? Are you able to identify with any examples from the case-studies in this chapter? Jules offers an interesting example of her exploration of the roots of her need to help. Her statement, 'I still get the urge with clients to make it OK', highlights significant issues for a counsellor who experiences the need to help. It may be difficult for a counsellor who is struggling, or unaware of this need to help, to offer their client a safe environment to struggle with their issues. In this situation, the counsellor may unwittingly try to protect the client from experiencing their difficulties and the pain of attempting resolution.

• Martha highlights her discovery, 'it was a need to do something for me, to help others for my own self-worth'. Martha has recognised that one of her own needs is to help others and within this process she experiences a valuing of her self. She has identified that she wants to help others, to help herself.

• It may take you until the end of training to be able to honestly answer this question.

• The question of need or want to help may also lead you to explore your motivation for training as a counsellor. In some ways this may be a much more straightforward question to consider — what *really* is your motivation? Why do you want to embark on counselling training?

• What is it about you that makes you think you will make an effective and competent counsellor?

• What is your background knowledge of counselling and how does this impinge on your motivation? After a counselling session, Paul had the 'clarity of vision to realise [he] needed to embark on full-time counselling training . . .'

points to ponder

3

why (and how) I chose person-centred counselling training

BAC and other organisations maintain a difference in definition between 'professional counselling' (where the title *counsellor* is formally used), and 'counselling skills', which are used to supplement another activity or profession, such as befriending, teaching or nursing. So the use of counselling skills may be a *part* of the job of nursing and teaching, but the nurse or teacher would not be qualified to call themselves a 'counsellor'.

There are three questions covered within this chapter;
1. Why does someone want to train as a counsellor?
2. Why might they choose the Person-Centred Approach to counselling?
3. How does anyoneone choose a specific training course?

There are many different reasons why people choose to train as counsellors. (Which is slightly different from the *motivation* to get into counselling featured in Chapter 2.) One route can be the result of personally experiencing a difficult, emotional or physical trauma. In this situation an individual is faced with the experience of a range of perhaps new feelings and has to find a way of addressing their situation. We do this in different ways, maybe through talking to friends, family, a counsellor, priest, someone in the helping professions etc. Or using expressive or creative therapeutic alternatives such as writing, art, reading, physical exercise, music etc. These ways of coping can put us in touch with our feelings, and help us as we try to understand why we feel the way we do, and perhaps feel less alone in our suffering. Some of the case-studies identified past 'traumas' as a starting point. They speak of the learning that has been gained from personal experiences and the desire to pass on the positive benefits experienced by feeling listened to and understood.

Counselling is often a development or extension of a person's job, perhaps a skill which supports them in their job, such as in the ministry, teaching, nursing, or in management. Counselling-style helping is used in a variety of occupations, whether formally or informally. Many trainees explain that their decision to embark on training comes from the awareness of their increasing involvement with people and resulting sensitive issues. They may remain in their profession offering counselling without the formal job title of 'counsellor'. Sometimes the individual chooses to move directly into the counselling profession. Many enrol on *counselling skills courses* to learn how to offer a different way of relating to people in their work environment. In this way, counselling skills have applicability in every work environment. Such skills teach us to listen, to relate and to communicate better. Clearly these benefits can easily transfer to our home-life as well. Often it is a combination of factors which bring us to training and exploring the world of counselling.

It felt a natural choice for Laura to focus on person-centred counselling rather than an alternative approach. She had limited experience of psychodynamic, cognitive and behavioural approaches. In seeing these approaches used, Laura was often left with the feeling of the client being 'done to'. It appeared to her that the client was being told how to deal with his/her problem. Laura's impression is based on only a few practitioners and is not a comprehensive reflection on these approaches. In addition to this, Laura's rejection of people 'being done to' stems from a personal experience of receiving medical treatment as a child and as a result feeling distinctly like an object. A combination of both factors was enough to send Laura in the direction of person-centred counselling. She related immediately to the approach and knew that she wished to pursue it further. It felt like a natural path for her to explore.

It may feel difficult to decide whether or not a particular counselling approach is suited to your personality and way of viewing the world. To help in your search, we will describe the fundamental principles of person-centred counselling. This may allow you some food for thought as to whether or not the approach fits your values.

The core tenet of person-centred counselling is that the counsellor believes that each individual (including the counsellor themselves) has an innate ability to develop and grow despite the conditions they may be experiencing. In a counselling setting, this belief means that the counsellor will trust their clients' own path of development and their own ability to make the right choices for their way of living.

Carl Rogers called this innate drive to develop and grow, despite the situation, the *actualising tendency*. He describes a childhood story which captures the essence of this belief:

> *I remember that in my boyhood the potato bin in which we stored our winter supply of potatoes was in the basement, several feet below a small basement window. The conditions were unfavourable, but the potatoes would begin to sprout — pale white sprouts, so unlike the healthy green shoots they sent up when planted in the soil in the spring. But these sad, spindly sprouts would grow two or three feet in length as they reached the distant light of the window* (Kirschenbaum, H. and Henderson, V. L. (Eds) 'The Carl Rogers Reader', 1994, p. 380, London: Constable).

Rogers understood that despite a difficult environment which tries to oppress growth, the potatoes (and indeed all organisms) demonstrate that they can grow. This gave him the idea that every organism (including, importantly, human beings) has this ability to make the best of their environment. This, as described above, is known in person-centred counselling as the *actualising tendency*. Person-centred counsellors hope to mobilise the actualising tendency by providing the conditions required for healthy growth. This is the second part of Rogers' theory in which he describes these conditions. In training to be person-centred counsellors we learn about the three conditions which the counsellor offers to the client to create a therapeutic environment for that client. Described by Carl Rogers in the late 1950s, these building-blocks of successful counselling are known as the *core conditions*, and are: *empathy*, *unconditional positive regard* and *congruence*. The counsellors' awareness of the core conditions are explored, tested and developed during training.

It is not the intention of this chapter to discuss the core conditions at great length but to offer a general view as to why trainees chose this approach. Clearly the theory and practice will represent much of what attracts people to this approach. For a more detailed explanation, several definitive books are listed in Appendix 2. However, the case-studies refer to the core conditions and it may be helpful to have a quick definition to help aid understanding.

Empathy is the counsellor's effort to feel a deep understanding of the client and their world, and to communicate this understanding to the client. The counsellor's understanding is rooted in the client's perception of their own experience and not the counsellor's. In simple terms this means trying to put yourself in the other person's place, or 'walking in their shoes'. This may sound simple enough but it involves the counsellor understanding themselves sufficiently to be able to recognise their own feelings as distinct from those of their client.

Unconditional positive regard is often known as *acceptance* or *non-judgemental warmth*. In offering unconditional positive regard, the counsellor is showing the client that she accepts them as a person. The counsellor does not have to experience the same values or behaviour as the client to offer this unconditional positive regard. The counsellor is accepting the client's right to their own feelings and actions. The counsellor is not attempting to change the client but offers the client an environment of open warmth and acceptance. In this environment the client is able to look at themselves openly and honestly without fear of being judged.

Congruence is also sometimes known as *genuineness*. When a counsellor is being congruent they are offering the client a true reflection of their inner feelings and responses to the client's statement and behaviour. Other words used to describe this attitude are being *honest*, *real*, or sometimes, *transparent*. In other words, you are not concealing yourself in this therapeutic environment.

Consistent with each of these conditions is the need for the counsellor to continue in developing their own self-awareness to assist them to tune in accurately with their client. It may be that the person-centred counsellor is attempting to integrate these elements into their life as well as in the counselling room.

Appendix 2 provides a list of further reading which might help you learn about the other approaches.

Are you able to identify your personal philosophy to life and with other people? Can you see any common links between your personal philosophy and person-centred counselling? Understanding your approach to yourself and others may assist you in making the choice of appropriate therapeutic approach. Have you investigated any other therapeutic approach? Through understanding the general concepts of other approaches you may be able to understand more fully why a particular approach fits or does not fit for you.

BAC has a scheme whereby courses can become 'Accredited'. It is a 'kitemark' indicating the quality of the course — which will have fully qualified, experienced staff, a mimimum number of taught hours covering theory, practice, personal and professional development. There is more about course accredidation in the sidenote at the top of pages 63 and 104 and a list of Accredited courses can be obtained from BAC.

Finding the right course requires that you focus on practical issues as well as the philosophy of the course. You will need to consider issues of location, cost, duration and timing of the course. There may be several other questions you may wish to consider.
• Is the course you are looking at affiliated to a university or college, or validated by an awarding body?
• Is it accredited by the British Association for Counselling (BAC) or other professional body?
• Are any of these issues relevant to you?
• Will university affiliation/BAC Course Accreditation and/or external validation of the course assist you when seeking employment in counselling?

- How can you check out the credibility of the course?
- What level of qualification are you seeking (or is feasible in your circumstances) — Certificate, Diploma, Masters, Doctorate?

You should speak with the tutors and understand their background in counselling. A helpful source could be local counsellors and previous students of a course. You may also have to balance the degree of academic with experiential input you would prefer in a course. There are many factors involved in deciding which is the right course for you. If you are able to gather the relevant information you may feel more able to make an informed choice.

Rick wanted to train as a counsellor because he sought a new challenge. He 'tested the water' by enrolling on a local counselling skills course. This was fairly *eclectic* in its orientation but it did base itself on person-centred philosophies. However, Rick was also interested in several other therapeutic approaches — to him they all seemed equally valid and interesting. But practically speaking he had to be able to commute and he had limited savings to invest in training so he applied for, and was accepted on, a full-time Person-Centred Counselling Diploma course. To be honest if an alternative approach had been located nearby he probably would have gone for this. On reflection, he feels he made a good, if accidental, choice and he has no regrets at all. Rick feels he should have put in a bit more research than he did but ultimately he was restricted financially.

Teaching styles on counselling courses sometimes emphasise learning by doing (called experiential learning). Even though there is this emphasis of learning through your own experience, there is also a fair amount of theory to learn in a more straight-forward academic way.

Counselling courses can focus on one theoretical approach (such as *person-centred, psychodynamic, Gestalt* etc.) or they can draw on more than one approach, giving a flavour of each. These courses are known as *eclectic* or *integrative*.

Funding issues and money are covered in Chapter 18.

Wendy

I was disillusioned with nursing, the pay, the fast-tracking of patients, the lack of mental stimulation and was looking for a new direction. Due to personal circumstances, i.e. single parent, I would have been financially worse off working and thus am on benefits and living at home. However, I am looking to a career for the future, for when my children are older and I am sure that counselling is for me. I have always been a good listener and the one that friends confide in and come to in times of trouble. I have undergone many difficult times myself which helps me empathise more easily. The Person-Centred Approach is one which follows three core conditions, where a counsellor offers empathy, unconditional positive regard and congruence to a client within the therapeutic relationship. It is a very people-focused or people-orientated approach and one which frankly simply fits well with how I feel I am as Wendy.

Dave

My route into person-centred counselling training was both impulsive and considered. I saw an advertisement for a counselling course at a certain university which sounded a fascinating course in a lovely part of the country. But I knew nothing of the subject. I was also doubtful whether my living in another part of the country would make me ineligible. However, subsequent enquiries showed that I would be and I decided to apply. In this way the Person Centred Approach chose me. Had the university followed a different counselling philosophy I daresay I may still have made efforts to get in.

Daniel   After I finished my Post Graduate Certificate in Education, I was approached to teach counselling skills by an adult education centre. My previous background is in working with the head-injured and their families. Here I worked as an unsupervised counsellor amongst a whole variety of other roles. The courses that I began to teach were so popular that I began to teach a Certificate in Counselling. As I had developed my own thirst for learning and was also now working in a supervised practice of my own, I decided that I should follow the rules and get the appropriate qualifications which would give me some counselling credibility, I therefore applied to do an Advanced Diploma at a prestigious college about ten miles away from my home. However, they would not admit me onto the Diploma because I did not have a qualification at Certificate level, even though I was teaching a Certificate in Counselling and already had experience! I did not mind as I felt it would be advantageous to start at the bottom and work my way up and that I would learn a lot that would be useful for my course.

Generally I was drawn into counselling training for four reasons. Firstly, probably *Iggi* for a need to make some sense of my own life. Secondly, I was fascinated by the psychology of the process of counselling and, thirdly, I wanted to become 'professional' in some way and counselling seemed like a worthy root. Finally, I wanted to offer something back to 'society' for help that I had received in the past. With regards to choosing the Person-Centred Approach, I felt this philosophy reflected my own needs as a client seeking understanding. This needed to be within my own terms of the meaning and temporal development not someone else's framework. It was to do with being unconstrained by a structured doctrine or process.

Vicki   It was about two years after we had hit our crisis, and things were improving, that I first became interested in counselling, coming from the perspective that if I could do anything to help people who found themselves in similar difficulties that we had faced, with noone to turn to, then I would. I did not want them to be as damaged as I felt I had been. This was my motivation towards counselling in its rawest sense, although I knew that this was not the time to become involved in counselling; I was too close to my own unhappiness. However, I did start training, going on a variety of short-term counselling courses, in fact any that were available at that time, and continued in this vein for about nine years. Then my husband noticed an advertisement for a six-week Introduction to Counselling course and suggested I go on it, which I did. I thoroughly enjoyed the experience. I knew that this was what I wanted to do next in my life. I had carried the desire for nine years and here was one way I could follow it fully. I felt our previous 'bad experience' was far enough in the past by then but my desire that other people should not have to suffer in the same way as I had still burned strongly.

The training they offered was eclectic, based on Carl Rogers' Person-Centred Approach to counselling. It was an approach with which I identified strongly. It offered acceptance and non-judgemental listening, something I had not been offered in the past. It valued people and placed trust and belief in them and I felt that this confirmed my own personal philosophy and value system.

Cathy   My choice of the field of counselling came from all my life experiences, educational background and my work with people in different settings. During the latter part of my school days, my visit to a career advisor, confirmed my inclination to follow a career in the helping professions. Child care and education, psychology, sociology and social work were subjects that kept me busy in my initial college education and search-for- work pursuits. Three years later, my career was still unclear and my personal life in an absolute turmoil. At the age of 21 I survived a serious suicide attempt and was left with some very strong impressions about the mental health professions.

Child psychology (a three-year course), which was my later selection, contributed to my realisation that I was on the right track. My enthusiasm and commitment to the course brought me to win two scholarships. At that time, I was greatly influenced by the Humanistic theory approach and fascinated by its optimism about human nature. I also grew an interest in anti-psychiatry. During the last year of my course, I studied, observed and practised 'Reality Therapy', a six-stage model developed by the American psychiatrist William Glasser, which challenged my way of thinking on self-responsibility and enabled me to think positively. By then, my fieldwork in a mental hospital, a residential home for young people, as well as my work in families with children was giving rise to my growing interest and motivation to pursue further professional training in counselling.

For a variety of reasons, taking decisive action was hard enough for both my husband and myself. Through the British Association for Counselling I found an accredited and humanistic course nearby. which was based on the work of Carl Rogers. I applied and was offered a place on the Certificate in Counselling Skills (part-time) for September 1991, which I accepted. I believe that my state of readiness for this new beginning was very well timed as I willingly made the course my high priority and my self-development central.

When I look back on my history of how I started to develop a person-centred way   *Annie*
of being, I clearly see how I was making an effort to actualise myself. I went into counselling training for a number of reasons. The way my mind works interested me and I wanted to concentrate on improving the quality of my life and relationships. Training in counselling seemed to me a great way of getting the intensity of focus I wanted. I wanted to learn about myself through learning about how other people functioned and actualised. I also wanted desperately to be self-employed. Bingo! I had found my ecological niche! All that remained was for me to set up home in it.

I set about researching counselling courses. I had heard about one from a friend who said the organisation had an excellent reputation. I did not want to go for the only one I'd heard about so I looked into a number of others. I went to an open evening here, a two-hour lecture there, got literature through the post etc. Then I discovered that the one with the 'excellent reputation' did a three-day introductory module. If I decided the course was for me, and they thought I was for them, that module would form the first of the eight foundation-year modules. I felt impressed. I went and stayed for five years whilst completing my Diploma.

Cari   The Person-Centred Approach is the only way that allows a client to draw upon their own abilities and to 'heal' themselves without losing touch with their essential uniqueness as an individual. Many would argue, I am sure, that other approaches do allow the client to use their own strengths. I do not deny that, but the Person-Centred Approach allows a person to become more themselves; the self which in other approaches seems often lost. Let me give you two brief examples from my experience to illustrate this:

In Psychoanalytic therapies, the client is actively encouraged to give away their power to the analyst and so to regress to an almost infantile state. If a client is unable to do this, they may be considered a failure by the analyst and so their self-image is diminished by the experience.

In some of the Cognitive/Behavioural approaches, a client is required to concentrate on thoughts and behaviours aside from emotion and, as with the psychoanalytic therapies, is required to fit into a particular mould, implemented by the therapist. If the client is unable to work in this particular way they may once again be perceived, or may perceive themselves, as a failure.

Person-centred counselling, however, allows the client to come just as they are, warts and all, to work through whatever they want, in the way that they can. It is my job as a therapist to fit into their framework, to accept them for who and what they are and bring. Now before my colleagues from other schools of thought get upset, I am not saying that their approaches are wrong — they can be a very effective way of working with certain clients at particular times. After all, I work within a Cognitive/Behavioural framework for much of the time because it is the most suitable way of working with many of my client group. There is, however, something very special about the person-centred way of working that can enable and empower clients to become more fully themselves, to use pastoral terminology, to become the person God intended them to be, not the person I, their family, their church or society says that they 'should' be. This is what I liked about this approach and was the reason I sought counselling training in this framework.

Jackie

From a skills training course I had identified very clearly that for me a person-centred framework was the framework which felt most 'me' — that Carl Rogers had given a name to something I was practising already. That this was the framework I would most like to explore more fully — along with a desire to learn more from other theories too. It felt the framework with most respect for people's autonomy and most trust in how we live (always self-actualising).

Jenny   I met a friend of a friend who was a Transactional Analysis Counsellor and who ran a short course on counselling skills. I chatted to her about counselling and she gave me addresses to follow up, as by this time I was beginning to wonder what career direction to take. Another strand to this is that I met my husband-to-be when abroad. He usually lived and had a flat in a city in the UK which boasted a BAC Accredited counselling diploma course. As I had had no formal counselling skills training, I thought I was being slightly ambitious applying for the Diploma and I fully expected to be told to do a skills course first. However, I also felt that my experiences had amply replaced any formal training.

I knew nothing about the Person-Centred Approach, although my sister sent me 'On Becoming a Person' by Carl Rogers. I would say that the approach chose me rather than the other way round! I did feel, however, that the approach corresponded to my own positive view of human nature.

Having obtained an RSA Certificate in Counselling Skills on a Transpersonal course and a Certificate in Counselling Theory, I was able to identify myself and my beliefs most with person-centred concepts. And I wanted a course which equally combined theoretical learning with experiential learning, believing these to be intrinsically inseparable needs in both training and the ongoing development of a good practising counsellor. It is for this reason I chose such a course. I was not disappointed.

Carrie

Charlie

My choice of course was very much influenced by the courses available in the local area. Also I wanted to do a BAC recognised course if at all possible. I didn't really know a great deal about the different orientations of counselling and so I can't really say that I made a positive decision to do person-centred counselling rather than another approach.

I chose my particular course for several reasons; it named issues which would be accommodated, it had an accessible venue, it had skills courses for black students only, which fed into diploma level courses, and had fee remission for people on low incomes. It meant a long physical journey for me but I felt so relieved at interview that these issues were on somebody's agenda . . . and it was a person-centred course. I wouldn't necessarily be learning only alongside people already in the field or with money for what *can* be an expensive training programme. I can't help how important that has felt for me.

Brian

Radnor

I went to see a counsellor when I broke up with my partner. I was also thinking of a career change. The counsellor continually asked about my relationship with my parents and aspects of my childhood. This really irritated me. I wanted to be listened to. I needed space to sort things out. I didn't need someone to make cognitive interpretations about something which seemed totally irrelevant. Much of this experience fed into my eventual choice, not only to train in counselling but to do so in a person-centred way.

points to ponder

See Appendix 2 for further recommended reading.

Many people want to improve their personal and professional relationships, do some voluntary work or develop a skill to use alongside their job (if they are a teacher or nurse) without 'going all the way' and qualifying to become a professional counsellor. It might be a good idea to enrol on a *counselling skills* or *intermediate course* to 'test the water' and find out how far you really want to (or need to, for career purposes)pursue counselling training.

• Why are you choosing the Person-Centred Approach? The case-studies reveal a range of motivations and reasons for choosing this particular approach. Wendy was 'disillusioned', Dave 'impulsive and considered', Daniel wanted to 'follow the rules' and Iggi lists four reasons. He wanted to 'make sense of his life', he was 'fascinated by the process of counselling', he 'wanted to become professional in some way' and wanted to 'offer something back to society'.

• The Person-Centred Approach is probably the most popular one in the UK at present. However, this does not necessarily mean or imply that it is easier to get a job at the end of training. There may be some employers who have a preference for, say, a Gestalt therapist, or someone who has trained along Cognitive Behavioural lines.

• Have you considered other approaches, such as Gestalt Therapy, Transactional Analysis, Cognitive Behavioural Approaches, Rational Emotive Behavioural Therapy, Psychodynamic Approaches, Solution-focused or Brief Therapy? The list will probably sound confusing and endless to you especially when you are just thinking about starting counselling training. Ask around, try reading a simple introduction and then see how the philosophies behind these approaches sound to you. Do any of them fit in with your way of looking at the world?

• The Person-Centred Approach is not necessarily the easiest. This approach does not put any emphasis on being *analytical* or an expert. Being an expert can sometimes be very attractive to some people, whilst others prefer a more egalitarian approach where the client is seen as their own expert.

• Can you connect with the 'feelings' side of you? This is a core element of the Person-Centred Approach. Or are you a 'thinker' or 'analyser'? If you are one of the latter two, like many who choose the Person-Centred Approach, it doesn't mean you are unsuitable but it may mean that it might be more difficult for you than someone who naturally can get in touch with or be more attuned to their feelings.

• Training is expensive, financially and emotionally. It can be a great cost to embark on training in a particular approach that becomes inappropriate for you or incompatible with your own goals and aspirations.

• There are a small number of people who do not complete a particular training course for a range of reasons. There are many more who, after training, do not become counsellors. In some instances this is because of the lack of jobs around and the number of trained counsellors competing for them. Some, however, discover that they do not want to become a counsellor and are content with the personal development benefits gained during training. For these people their training has also been a success.

• Would a course on counselling skills be sufficient or do you really feel the need and desire to go all the way?

To the uninitiated, 'personal development' may sound a rather intangible concept and in some ways it is. It refers to how we mature or grow, through our character, or personality — literally how we develop as persons. Much of this section will focus on two concepts; empowerment and self-awareness. Only a limited explanation will be given here because many of the subsequent case-studies provide very interesting interpretations of these concepts. Self-awareness has been mentioned previously, as Section A sought to highlight how and why people chose to embark on counselling training. We explained how some noticed a changing 'self-awareness' which sparked their interest in counselling. Personal development refers to the subsequent development of greater self-awareness.

Much of the testimony in this section speaks of the changes which happen during training. Throughout our lives we are experiencing changes and transitions which may relate to work, our family or our goals and these will all have an impact on us. Counselling training can accelerate this natural development process in many ways. It encourages us to question our views and beliefs on certain topics. We could go through our lives unaware that we are, for instance, racist but without challenge on this it may not become apparent. Training can provide a supportive environment where we can question ourselves and become aware of our attitudes.

Some readers will be familiar with the phrase 'emotional baggage' — the collection of side effects, fears, memories and habits we have accumulated from disagreeable experiences, or often, simply life itself. We all have some emotional baggage. 'Baggage' gives the impression or feeling of 'weight' and to some extent this is what emotional baggage means. For instance, we may have had a series of relationships which did not work out the way we wanted and we could be carrying round some of the negative or painful after-effects. Sometimes the unfavourable results of these broken relationships will tangle and frustrate our efforts to engage in future relationships. We may be left with the fear of failure, fear of rejection, or the desperate need for a successful relationship.

The end goal, of course, is to learn to be an effective counsellor. Counselling training may help us review what we have in the way of emotional baggage, offer us the opportunity to come to terms with this and help us to minimise the effect of this on our lives. The importance in having an emotional 'spring clean' is to ensure that we do not endanger a client-counsellor relationship with our own negative life experiences. Counselling is also a very effective mechanism with which we can deal with and enhance our personal development.

Many training courses have a separate course component called 'personal development'. On weekly courses, it will have a time slot every week of between one and two hours and is often run by a tutor who is not part of the course team and may be called a 'facilitator'. The title 'facilitator' is used to indicate that the personal development time is not like regular teaching and learning.

In other courses, there may be 'community time' which can be the place in which a fair amount of personal development takes place.

(If your objective is solely personal development, this route may be an expensive way to achieve this.) Personal development for its own sake might be better achieved through individual counselling, specific workshops, short courses or retreats specifically catering for self-development.

One of the most difficult challenges in life is concerned with relating to or interacting with people. The Person-Centred Approach places emphasis on the valuing of people, appreciating and accepting who they are, and much of the training will help us make best use of this focus. This will become the foundation on which we will learn how to be with people — another crucial part of personal development.

Chapter 4 looks at the 'process' of personal growth and development, i.e. the way in which people have achieved this or the manner, route or journey they have taken to help them develop themselves. The word 'process' is used frequently in counselling terminology. It refers to the *way* things happen and this is often a forward, progressive movement, but sometimes can be experienced as negative or painful. This chapter attempts to show through the case-studies how this *way* or 'process' can mean very different things to people — the speed and pace can differ, and some may need more time to synthesise or digest aspects of learning.

Chapter 5 looks at two key issues which are sometimes taboo subjects for some people — sexuality and spirituality. These topics can reveal much about who we are and how we act, think and feel. Many of our attitudes may be tied up with parental or social pressures but the focus of these topics within counselling training can be hugely illuminating for people. In many cases trainees may not have explored these subjects in any real depth before. However, what we may learn about ourselves can evoke powerful feelings as we discover the meaning that sexuality and spirituality have for us. In other words, we may see ourselves differently once we connect with a side of our personality which embraces a new spiritual and/or sexual dimension or allows us fully to experience an old one, maybe for the first time.

Chapter 6 covers personal counselling. Many trainees will find this an invaluable experience. It can be very useful, and some will say it is imperative, that we experience counselling from the position of being a client. Some might argue that this insight can aid our empathy skills, in the sense that we can understand how it is to be a client — the fears, apprehensions, concerns etc. The further benefit for the trainee counsellor is the opportunity to spend time reflecting on a particular concern or personal issue which may have been triggered off by course work, assignments, peers, tutors, family or any of a number of causes.

4
the
process of
personal
growth
and
develop-
ment

The process of personal growth and development is a fundamental concept to person-centred therapy. Personal growth and development, in relation to person-centred counselling, is a natural capacity to change and grow emotionally in a way that fits you as an individual. Person-centred counselling theory states that to move forward and grow is a natural tendency in all of us. In Carl Rogers' theory, this is referred to as the *actualising tendency* (Rogers, 1959).

However, in many of our lives this tendency may have been stunted or redirected to suit the social norms of our environment. The role of the counsellor is to provide a healing environment which allows the client to identify their natural way of developing and living and to trust this instinct.

You may be wondering what the term 'personal development' actually means. It can be quite difficult to define and summarise in a few words. This is due, in part, to the fact that personal development is different for everybody, but we will have a go.

So, in the first paragraph above, we mentioned that humans have a basic tendency to move towards fulfillment, and that is the startingpoint of our definition. To this we would add that personal development involves greater self-awareness (knowing more about who we are and how we think, feel and behave), a more personally appropriate set of values, beliefs and attitudes (what do we really value and find important in our lives?) and what are we striving to achieve (are our goals and ambitions compatible with realistic achievement?).

An environment that feels right and 'safe' for you is essential to allow you to begin the process of personal development. In the same way that a counsellor wishes to provide a safe environment for the client, a trainee is also seeking a place which will offer the right conditions for them to develop. Each of us may have a different idea of what makes a situation safe or not — indeed this is part of our development; recognising what is OK and what is not; recognising how to challenge and support ourselves and others. What we think makes an environment safe may change during the training period.

The core conditions of empathy, unconditional positive regard and congruence were discussed in the previous chapter and these are the conditions which we consider constitute a safe environment for personal development. As a trainee, one of the ways that you may learn is by observing the trainers' *way of being* i.e. how they portray and demonstrate these core conditions. Similarly, in order that your fellow trainees may experience your understanding, acceptance and genuineness, you may feel you want to be explicit and open with your feelings and actions. You may be unaccustomed to this, and you may find it difficult, challenging and painful, but also very rewarding.

Laura's previous experience of education was one of 'playing the game' and learning to fulfil the requirements of a particular course. It quickly became apparent that person-centred training does not work in this way. Laura learnt to respond to her own needs and question her own expectations. She began to wonder whether the expectations belonged to her or had she absorbed them from teachers, parents, peer group or partner. Laura learnt to dig for the true meanings of her reactions to situations. From this, she has a greater sense of stability and a clearer view of what is personally OK. Laura gained this from feeling able to experiment with her reactions and feelings in a non-judgemental environment.

Offering an environment in which personal growth and development are valued and encouraged works equally well in training as in therapy. Training encourages trainees to reflect on their level of self-awareness. By increasing your awareness, you will have a new option available — to move on and grow in a different way. Training provides the trainee with an environment which helps them to explore and start to understand their natural process.

The degree of personal development experienced is dependent on you, the individual. There will be many factors which will affect your state of readiness for personal development. You may be focused on a particular life-issue which limits your energy in other areas, for example, health, financial, work commitments and family, and your pace of development may alter throughout the training. If you are able to be aware of how you feel about yourself, maintaining a sort of internal dialogue with yourself and can make use of supervision and feedback with colleagues, hopefully you'll be able to understand your pace of development and work with it.

Since we do not change in isolation, personal growth and development can bring with it change which may be stressful to you and to people close to you. When we change, it is sometimes possible that those close to us may also change in relation to us. It can be an amazing feeling to see a stuck relationship or situation change as a result of self-development. Change, in this respect, is not as superficial as opting for a new hairstyle, for example, but more of an internal change — altering our values, deciding to modify our beliefs or learning, or fundamentally changing how we see things and how we behave.

Personal growth and development for Rick was like putting himself onto a track. He was aware that his particular training courses would help him understand more about himself but now sees this was very much a starting point. He began to see his development as a lifetime process and now he has a thirst for learning, for experiencing new things, for travelling, for meeting interesting people, for sharing his life with others, for enjoying himself and having fun — above all — for living.

In the case-studies you can hear the excitement in the voices of the trainees as they speak about the degree of learning and emotion they have experienced whilst training. You will read statements such as 'learning was mine'; 'inner development'; 'insight'; 'relative darkness on the inside'. The language of these statements is interesting. In these comments we hear a focus on learning, development, inner growth. The trainees' thoughts clearly illustrate the concept of personal growth and development.

Dwight   The learning in the early weeks was some of the greatest learning I have ever experienced, for it was mine. It opened the door quite early on to the realisation that I could learn from experience in a focused way and that I was different ,and I was excited. I looked forward to every moment for I had had the opportunity to light a fire inside me. From that ignition the course then provided fuel for growth and understanding, which was to become all mine. Some of this was going to come from 'prompts' from facilitators, presented by theories and situations but the learning was mine. Thirty-six people had joined in this room, thirty-six would leave with different learnings from each other about themselves. If each was prepared to take the risk!

I became a human being, no longer a clone of the system. Free to feel and express those feelings, seeming to be as if a light had been switched on, free to take what was being felt wherever I wished to go. Relating that human self that seemed to have been suppressed and yet certainly present. I was the person I am but I did not know me. I became more confident, open, alert, valuable.

I recall I wrote during my study time that there is almost 'a movement of imperceptible vibrations, a frequency almost unknown, not of any sound or light, not of any elements we hold as "real". But as though a flickering of a candle disperses a vibration in a field of connections between beings and creates a majesty of togetherness where we join'.

It has been this opening of my inner development that has been so valuable and satisfying. Not in the form of a religious experience, for we are all our own god. It is for us to behold that in ourselves, we are each able to be free to develop that personal freedom, not to be clones of those who have gone before. Part of my processing of understanding what has happened in the past has enabled me to realise that I have always been a 'people person'. Always attracted people, been warm to them. Only now do I see it, know it and satisfy from it.

I was surprised by the unenlightened or conservative views of some of my fellow   *Winnie*
students in areas such as race, sexual orientation and even appearance. I was equally amazed at the high level of personal growth of some students and wonder if any of them would say the same of me?

Ingrid   My personal development has been ongoing throughout the three-year course, though I gained significantly more insight in my final year. I developed a greater sense of my own individual experience and a respect for the experiences of others. I also felt myself becoming less judgemental and more respectful of the thoughts, feelings and beliefs of others (a growth in acceptance) whilst not losing sight of my own integrity.

The changes I experience in myself had a tremendous impact on my life, my way of thinking and behaving. I felt an improvement in myself of self, a greater autonomy and confidence. Finally, I believe I was able to see things with much greater clarity.

Cynthia

What really stands out in my mind now, for the three years that followed before finally moving back to London, was my personal struggle to cope with the painful and unfulfilled parts of myself. I believe it was some kind of preparation for my next journey, a journey of self-exploration and rediscovery. It seems to me that what followed, my three-year counselling training experience, was the beginning of the most important turning-point in my life. A distinct shift towards respect for my individuality and my capacities through understanding and accepting the meaning and value of my personal experiences as well as those of others.

Returning to training, I found the space and freedom to begin to self-explore, revealing more perceptions to my consciousness about myself and learning to stay with my experiencing in the present, allowing me to accept some of my feelings and share them with others when I chose to. I remember how impressed I was with my right to stay silent in the group and go at my pace without losing the respect and warmth of others. Through my experiencing of the core conditions [of empathy, congruence and unconditional positive regard — eds.], I was finding the courage to move deeper into my subjective area of self-knowledge. I once thought I knew myself well and by the end of that year I discovered I was in relative darkness on the inside. I knew I had a lot of work to do with myself and that was OK as I was feeling entitled to do it at my own personal pace. I believe in that year I grew in self-respect and became more sensitive and responsive to my own person, which started gradually to create turbulence in some of my personal relationships.

After the first term of that first year, my urge for self-exploration was becoming very powerful. Soon I realised that my conditional self's demand for perfection had outgrown its usefulness, which enabled me to move around with less fear to be myself and brought about a gradual loosening up of my deeper feelings, like my stored feeling of sadness. I also became more relaxed to appreciate and deal with my inner tensions and eventually made a more flexible learning agreement with myself that allowed me to develop my skills and accomplish the various tasks of the course in my own way.

After I qualified I encountered and confronted many difficulties whilst job-hunting for a part-time counselling psot which gradually flattened my inventiveness and excitement. I decided to have a break from my counselling work for some time and let myself crack under the strains of deep-seated issues which were of major importance to my development. It soon became clear to me that I had a greater struggle on my hands, that of giving serious thought about the quality of my relationship with myself, of experiencing a true present with myself for its own sake and contacting and trusting the intuitive side of my nature with regards to some events from the past. This has been a major shift in my process of self-change. In Rogers' terms, I am developing a strong internal locus of evaluation, and in my own words, I am doing the harvesting of the last six years — I am becoming more and more my own person.

Vicki   It was all right to be me, and what a revelation and relief that realisation gave me!!

I also learnt to say no and be more assertive and less of a doormat, not only in the *Wilma* relationship with my partner but in life in general, e.g. when faced with bad service in shops etc. However, this new assertiveness is tempered with empathy.

Chris   My first encounter with Carl Rogers' ideas and work awakened a new living potential, a different kind of learning for me, 'a learning from within'. Since then, I have been passionately engaged in exploring my life and experiences anew, realising the strength of my capacity to understand empathically and to trust my inner personal world. His writings touch me deeply, speaking 'to' me and 'for' me. I have perceived and acknowledged the reality of his ideas in both my personal and professional dimensions of life.

On the course I have felt inspired, frustrated, angry and moved in ways which I *Julie* feel a luxury. What a luxurious 'side effect' that an integral part of training in counselling is exploring myself.

Angie   Perhaps my most significant experience during my training was my growing realisation that everything I did fed into my personal development. My reading (both academic and recreational), my supervision, films, theatre, group discussion, 'check-ins' and 'check-outs' (times when we checked up on ourselves and each other for emotional support) my personal and professional relationships, and contact with my clients, all fed into, and were nourished by, each other. I felt tremendously excited by this phenomenon; I still do. I experienced my training as an intense process of self-examination and discovery from which I derived an enormous sense of spiritual fulfilment, entertainment and satisfaction.

I wanted to write something about empowerment because of its meaning to me. *Celia* Empowerment happens in two ways. If we are lucky we will be nurtured by parents or teachers as children and grow up with a strong sense of worth and value and a firm belief in our abilities. The majority of people, though, are not lucky, and then it is only when we have had our power forcibly removed from us that we can begin to seek to regain it in a new way. We only have to look at the examples from people living under any form of repression to find empowered individuals; Paulo Friere, living under a repressive regime, though his experiences was able to firstly become empowered and then seek ways to empower others. Other examples include Nelson Mandela, Martin Luther, Emily Pankhurst and Oscar Romero. They each risked their lives and their liberty to become 'subversives' in their need to free others from those who had *power* over them.

The majority of us, unlike these people, do not live under repressive regimes, yet we still have in many ways experienced a considerable loss of power to others, through, for instance, abuse (physical and sexual) and other forms of violence. Also through less obvious situations of powerlessness, where we are belittled, bullied, ignored, constantly criticised or never affirmed. These can be equally destructive and damaging.

It is, then, from the depths of these experiences that we can begin to feel empowered, either by someone close to us, a counsellor, or from our innate sense of justice and freedom. It is as if it is our own brokenness that helps us to enable others, even when our wounds do not seem as deep or as painful as those brought to us by our clients. Once we have become empowered it is then that it gets hard. My own journey through counselling was at times very painful, confronting the demons within but I came through the pain and use it to help others. What makes it hard ,now, is other people — they do not like to think that you might be empowering someone close to them. As counsellors we have to learn to deal with this not only for ourselves but for our clients and those close to them. It is worth the struggle!

At this point I would like to throw a small spanner in the works and say that it is my belief that it is very difficult to empower other people without having been empowered ourselves.

Eileen　　　　For me the course was a rollercoaster of emotions during the first year. I felt superior to many of the other students, then completely incompetent and unsuitable to be a counsellor at all. I realised I used my ability to work on myself as a defence and resented authority whilst trying to please it. This meant I was reluctant to really let my counselling work be 'truly seen' in essays and was constantly disappointed during that first year when my written work did not receive a credit. By the start of the second year after personal, peer and tutor assessments, I was able to come to terms with these issues. I relaxed, became more confident, less aggressively confrontational with my fellow students and developed a deep belief in myself whilst still remaining willing to look at myself, my practice and challenge others when I felt the *congruent need*.

And I did begin to speak. Actually, I began to roar. And I found that as I became more myself, and spoke that self, and lived that self, the more alive others became, and I then lived further. I found utter delight in their difference to me and our speaking with each other. But that is too calm, too academic, too seated.　　　*Kenny*

After time together, we embrace. Our touch, our hugs, our kisses take our realities beyond words. All I can do is write that it is like swimming for the first time in the warmth of Atlantic waves, being sucked and pulled and diving through and dancing in the depths of the waters. It is like the shimmer of a bowl stained deep blue, glowing on a plain wooden table.

And as I knew myself, I felt myself go back through so many pasts to find myself, to know my location. That this is my identity in these places, and why and how, and not be frightened by what I found, but to know. I knew my roles and I knew something of how I could be with some kind of wholeness, enough integrity to know myself that I was alive — and acceptable to me.

And this is something about expectation. Not to get through academic hoops but to know that there is a chance that on a counselling course the student might even find parts of themselves they did not know existed and explode with the joy of that knowledge and weep for the years spent walking in the valleys of death.

Donal   My training had a dramatic effect on me. A disability I have still, though now insignificant, is a stammer. From not being able to say my name to working as a telephone counsellor is pretty staggering to me. Earning money via my mouth!

My training experience was not about learning techniques or even skills in any   *Agnetha*
recognised sense of the word. It was about learning who and what I am. I trained myself to feel freer and to be able to offer other people an environment where they could learn to feel freer too. I experienced my own organismic impulse to grow, develop and achieve my potential.

• You must be ready or receptive to experience personal change during training — change in your beliefs, attitudes, values and perceptions.

• 'Change' can be frightening because it may open up something new. It is something we are not used to and may take time to settle. It seems to be a common human trait that we are resistant to change. In many cases it is a *fear* of change rather than the change itself. However, life is all about change — we may move house, get married, change jobs and many more smaller but no less significant transitions.

• Some types of change can upset our relationships with friends and family, colleagues at work etc. Wilma's case-study highlights the impact of her personal growth through training. She says, 'I also learnt to say no and be more assertive and less of a doormat, not only in that relationship with my partner but in life in general.'

• Change can be the best thing that's ever happened to us. Ingrid demonstrates this clearly through her views 'The changes I experience in myself had a tremendous impact on my life, my way of thinking and behaving. I felt an improvement in myself of self, a greater autonomy and confidence. Finally, I believe I was able to see things with much greater clarity.'

points to ponder

• Change can also be the worst thing that's happened to us. For example, we may decide to make a career change into a new area only to find that this change was not appropriate and that the original career was more suitable. The case-studies in this chapter focus on former trainees highlighting the positive learning which they have taken from their struggles with change. Is this a common trait in individuals who train in counselling? Or is it a trait of trainees attached to the Person-Centred Approach?

• You are likely to get to know yourself more. This means you will know how and why you react to different comments, situations and issues. You may discover new areas of your personality which were visible to others but hidden to you. The trick is to continue with your process of change and self-awareness. This will assist you in the recognition of your reactions and feelings and also of the potential acceptance of these previously 'hidden' areas. You may also discover new things about yourself that you dislike.

5
spirituality
and
sexuality

In this chapter we have linked two fundamental elements of being human — spirituality and sexuality. The chapter offers a selection of the personal views of former trainees to illustrate the unique impact these issues have had upon them. It is clear that there is no one 'correct' way of viewing or defining either spirituality or sexuality. Because of the complex and inherently different meanings for everyone, these tend to be difficult areas for people to pinpoint specific issues and feelings. This may explain, to some extent, why so few of our contributors have chosen to write on these issues.

Some people make a definite distinction between religion and spirituality but for others they are inextricably connected, and this divergence is represented in the testimonies. However, as reported by our respondents, common to both views seems to be the belief that spirituality is linked to a sense of intimacy.

For Laura, spirituality is about her understanding and belief of herself and others, in relation to each other and how they fit into the natural world. To her, spirituality is about connection to ourselves, physically and emotionally, connection to others and connection to our environment. For her, the development of her spirituality came with her increased exploration of these issues in her life and linking them together. She became aware of an inter-relatedness between herself, others and her environment. Allowing her feelings and ideas to flow from one to the other allowed her to develop a greater sense of herself and her place in the world.

Sexuality for Laura concerns her emotional and physical response to herself, and herself in relation to others.

We can embrace or reject our sexuality in many different ways. There may be parts of our sexuality which remain hidden from others and at times from ourselves. As counsellors it is important that we try to understand our sexuality and our responses and attraction to others. If we do not understand this, we risk confusing ourselves and our clients or rejecting them through fear of not understanding why we are responding to them in a particular way.

To some readers it may seem unusual to see spirituality and sexuality placed together in a chapter. We believe, however, that there are commonalities, for example, for many people there is a high degree of intimacy involved in each. For others, in both spirituality and sexuality, the individual is in relationship *with* self, others and their environment. These commonalities suggest a fluidity in both sexuality and spirituality. Perhaps this also suggests that both require a

Gay, lesbian and bisexual people may be worried that they will experience the same discrimination and oppression in their training that they suffer in society at large. It is true to say that experiences vary, and there is some writing that you might find useful, particularly Dominic Davies and Charles McNeal's *Pink Therapy* (the title shoud speak for itself) — details in Appendix 2.

Also of interest will be Michele Crouan's article in *Counselling* (February 1996) *Pushing Against the Wind: the recognition of lesbians in counselling training.*

Counselling is the journal of the BAC. Ask at your local library or contact BAC (see Appendix 3) to find out how to get hold of a copy of this article.

sense of faith and trust in self and others.

An additional aspect of both spirituality and sexuality is the potential 'hidden' quality. It seems possible for an individual's sense of sexuality and spirituality to be hidden from themselves and others. It may be that this is an active choice made due to external social pressures. Or it may be that there is a lack of awareness by the individual in relation to these areas. Before we are prepared to share our fears and experiences of spirituality and sexuality, many of us will need a safe environment and a high degree of trust, especially when an issue is hidden from the outside world or ourselves. Lesbian, gay and bisexual people may reasonably fear that training groups will not accept them and their sexuality. (Since the 'outside world' is homophobic, why should a person-centred training course be any different?) We would hope that the honest, accepting and supportively challenging environment that a person-centred training course should offer would be just the right space for everyone to begin exploring these issues.

If it wasn't for his counselling training, Rick's attitude towards, and personal understanding of, his sexuality and spirituality would have remained in the 'dark ages'. He had never properly explored, what became to him, massive dimensions of sexuality before and discovered that he had been quite homophobic in the past. He was able to explore why this was the case and discovered that much of this was due to ignorance. The most insightful learning came after he finished his diploma in counselling course. With a majority of women on the course and as many gay men as heterosexual men, he had focused on *feelings* and *emotions* so much that it had pushed him into being a person with an equal masculine and feminine side. Latterly, Rick's concept of sexuality is to appreciate and respect the fact that he is a man. He is in touch with his 'feminine' side, but first and foremost he's a man.

In terms of spirituality, Rick sees this as a philosophy of life rather than a construct of a particular religion or divine belief. He believes in a god and aspires to a moral code of conduct and being. Aware of the richness of doctrinal diversity from different cultural communities, Rick's aim is to respect them all.

I began to react ever more strongly towards the power abuses of the church. Working for the church, my belief in the Christian God began to be unbearable. I left. Our lives (mine and my partner's) have been turned upside down. I have the security of what was and, for most, still is a job for life. I have begun to find something of a life.

Korin

Death came when I felt labelled as the 'course's psycho'. The madness I was experiencing was a full-scale evocation and retelling of being broken by an institution (the church) which spoke one thing and did another. And that process of being broken was not heard by the course, nor responded to, except in laying the responsibility upon me. After all, the client is, ultimately, responsible for themselves. We are responsible to, not for, our clients.

> **Molly** I can't give you the full monty as regards to my experiences without reliving the stress of my Diploma, except to note or point out how much of me was touched at depth with regards to the hours we spent on *spirituality*. I feel it is important to nurture all aspects of our being.

My training led me to make a differentiation between religion and spirituality. By my understanding the former tends to promote or stand for a doctrinal membership group. The latter is a state of being, a process of belief and free in terms of 'membership', application and interpretation. I feel we develop and define our spirituality as the inner part of who we are. This then forms our beliefs and values. **Michael**

> **Victoria** The subject matter I chose for my dissertation was on spirituality, with particular reference to Carl Rogers' Person-Centred Approach to counselling. It was during the writing of this that my Christian faith, although it had been part of me for a very long time, became totally integrated with my counselling work. It was as if the two areas of my faith and my work had been made for each other, had been made to fit together. It all made sense, and as I pointed out in my dissertation, the model which Carl Rogers had developed fitted very closely with the model Jesus offers us in the Gospels, the model that Christianity in its truest form is based on. Sadly the Jesus model seems to be often twisted and skewed to fit man's need to make himself feel better at the expense of others through criticism and judgementalism, which I suppose is where the dogmatic attitude comes from that the Christian Church is often criticised for. Nevertheless, a lot of things fell into place for me at that time and I felt very positive and more integrated than I ever felt before.

I have always been in touch with both my sexuality and my spirituality but now this is more mature and better understood, respected and appreciated. I now do not let either become an escape from reality but let them integrate into the whole experience of being me, Isla. **Isla**

> **Klaus** I have always found that my sexuality is an instrument of raging hate, desiring lust and even a sweet loving. And I have found that even words carry the power and gentleness, dignity and slobbery of an eroticism. I am aware that whenever I work at depth, these simple realities are present. They are friends I walk with when I walk with clients.

I was single throughout my training. I suppose there was the benefit that I did not have a partner to confuse and alienate during this process! But I got the downside big time. I was deeply touched by the closeness of intensity and intimacy provided by my colleagues. So much so, that I can honestly say that I fell in love, partly with a couple of my peers and in a strange sense with the collective group. It was a different love for each, but very real, very strong and a powerful force which nearly suffocated me. This felt to me to be my expression of my sexuality, the **Michael** recognition that I had a sexual response and I was energised or triggered by this love. And this was a big thing for me, exploring love and sexuality. For me I began to find the strong connection between the two. Sexuality is something to do with my identity and exposes who I am as an individual and impacts on how I communicate and relate to others. Love is a concept which flows from my sexuality. I also had a fascinating time considering the platonic dimension of my sexuality, which initially seemed a strange paradox.

> ***Gordon***   Is it not the Chinese who have some 20 words to describe various aspects of love? I can and have experienced many more meanings and again this is all tinged to some degree with our sexuality, I think. 'I'm too sexy for my love . . .', well, it's something like that!

I found the exploration of spirituality and sexuality a fascinating topic. Not only did I learn so much about myself and others but I felt a connection between the two. As deep internal aspects of who we are, spirituality and sexuality seem to me to be intertwined, they are constructs which portray the existential component of me, Fi.   *Fi*

> ***Steph***   I'm still not quite sure which of these two topics has had the most influence on me. Both seem to be completely cocooned in expectations from family and society. Our meaning of sexuality is borne by our parents. I felt that my parents had overprotected me because I was an only child. The effect of this was that I was very self-conscious about developing into a woman during my youth. Now in my forties, I'm aware I still have hang-ups. This annoys me because it seems that whatever this parental mollycoddling was about, it has stunted my own growth as a person. My counselling training helped me free this up, so much so that I can say that my way of dressing has changed! I feel more of a woman now!
>
> In terms of spirituality much the same occurred. My parents went to church and so I did too. It was what they did, so there was little questioning about this. It seemed this was expected of me. Later on I went to boarding school and dropped my links to the church, mainly because I could. I've since come back in touch with a more spiritual understanding of religion. I'm an Episcopalian now and do go to church. Now this is on my terms, not my parents, not society's but mine.

points to ponder

- Like it or not, sexuality and spirituality will almost certainly come up during training and in your work as a counsellor.

- Trainees often find these subjects to be amongst the most significant stages of their training. They are at the core of who we are. By exploring these areas, ultimately we are attempting to understand fundamental aspects of our personality and who we are.

• Sexuality and spirituality are important areas to all of us. Some of us may already be actively exploring one or both areas. Our values and beliefs regarding these are linked to our exposure to life events and self-awareness. For many of us this may be linked to early life experiences, family values, local community, media, education and peer group influences etc.

• Some of us will have positive, and others will have negative, experiences of spirituality. From the case-studies we can see that Korin reacted 'even more strongly towards the power abuses of the church'. However, Molly mentioned how much of her was 'touched at depth with regards to . . . spirituality'. Steph talks about the 'negative' influence of family and society on her evolving understanding of her own sexuality and spirituality. To what extent has society, the family or the media altered your beliefs, values and attitudes?

• We may use a variety of ways to express our sexuality and spirituality. A connection between sexuality and spirituality is described well by Isla who claims she does not 'let either become an escape from reality but let[s] them integrate into the whole experience of being [her]'.

• Very few of us come to counselling training with a clear idea of what sexuality and spirituality really means to us. It may take a lifetime to get anywhere near a clear explanation for ourselves. Furthermore, as humans we are continually evolving and changing — our views today may be quite different from those five years ago and five years hence.

• In our normally shy and bashful culture it is enlightening to hear of Klaus's awareness, describing his sexuality as 'an instrument of raging hate, desiring lust and even a sweet loving'.

If you are (or think you will be) particularly interested in counselling and spirituality, we have suggested a couple of books looking at spirituality and the Person-Centred Approach in the further reading section in Appendix 2.

6
support
and the
need for
personal
counsel-
ling

What does personal counselling mean to you? Is it about seeing a counsellor if a particular problem arises, using the process of counselling to identify the difficulties and a way of dealing with them? Is it about increasing your understanding regarding personal relationships? Is personal counselling something that you would actively choose for yourself? Is it a choice which feels natural in your life? Or is it a prospect which would come from the suggestion of someone else? Is it an idea that you would actively seize and carry out?

For Laura, personal counselling gave her the time and space to understand and learn to accept how she felt about herself and how she was with others. For others it might be about ongoing personal development and self-exploration.

You will have to come to an understanding of your views on personal counselling. It doesn't necessarily follow that because you wish to counsel others that you would be happy to be counselled personally. If this is the case you may wish to consider why. Laura is interested in this aspect because she initially felt this way. She felt able to counsel others but was reluctant to enter into a counselling relationship as a client, so she tried to understand why. She felt scared, unable to shake the feeling that she was about to open a can of worms that she would have no control over. Once in counselling, however, Laura realised that, in person-centred therapy, the pace of change and understanding was hers and not dictated by the therapist. In reality, it was her *fear* of the process and the areas she wished to look at that were controlling her.

When thinking about your attitude towards training, do you feel that experiencing personal counselling may have an impact on your counselling approach with your client? It may assist you in understanding the counselling process experienced by the client. It may be helpful to be in the 'other chair' for a number of reasons — to experience what it's like to be really listened to, to become aware of the counsellor's rapport, to struggle for our self-understanding and to see how someone else works.

Each training course has its own set of criteria which you will be required to meet in order to complete your training. It is important that you understand and agree with the criteria. It may be that the course criteria require you to experience a set number of personal counselling sessions. Do you feel that experiencing personal counselling is *essential* to your understanding of the process of counselling?

Rick found personal counselling invaluable. It gave him an insight into what an experience of person-centred counselling was like. In some ways he became frustrated because he was often distracted by the anticipation a 'person-centred response'! He was checking out his counsellor although he's aware that this was probably an expensive use of the time. He did find he could use the space to explore issues which were only briefly touched on during the training so in a way it was a crucial follow-through of the training process. Now, Rick cannot understand how anyone can become a counsellor without having experienced this for themselves.

Danny

Never had I experienced or considered personal counselling prior to this course. It was actually part of the suggested criteria and would have happened anyway, I feel. How could I be with someone on a journey of understanding if I had not experienced that for myself?

Victoria

For a couple of main reasons, I decided about halfway through the second year to undertake personal counselling. Firstly, how people saw me, how they thought of me affected me too much. Secondly, some material about my mother (who had died four years previously) came out in the context of the Personal Development Group. My counsellor was person-centred and I felt so valued, heard and understood that I continued working with her for 18 months.

I began another series of personal counselling sessions last summer. Again, I will probably continue for about 18 months. This time my therapist is more Pychodynamic/Gestalt and I have found my sessions with her both challenging and very stimulating. She has been encouraging me towards more practical challenges in the interpersonal aspects of my life and, as a result, my sense of safety has been growing and developing to a much deeper sense of congruence within myself.

Julia

A couple of weeks into the second term I felt the need to explore issues which had emerged in the Personal and Professional Development Groups more fully and so I contacted a personal counsellor. This was a big step for me, as it was not something I had ever envisaged myself doing. It also had to be talked through very carefully with my husband as he was initially fearful that my seeking counselling reflected somehow a lack in him or in our relationship.

Michael

I sought personal counselling towards the end of my full-time one-year Diploma course for a number of reasons. I felt I had engaged well in and used effectively the various support groups on the course but there were a couple of issues that I thought I needed more time to deal with and reconcile. One related to my relationship with my father who, over the 40 years of my life, I came to the conclusion had been absent for much of my early life. This *absent* father had had a negative effect on me in terms of how I related to men in general and people as authority figures. The second part of my counselling was based on holding me together emotionally from the effects of the preceding months on the course. The course was hugely intensive and almost became a checklist of seminars and workshops on every topic of 'being a human being'. While it was hugely interesting and useful, the array of subjects we covered seemed to impact on me deeper and deeper as the training progressed and I opened myself up to the various aspects of experiencing and working with them. I had opened myself up to the many facets of sexuality, my childhood experiences, death, past relationships, relating to people etc. and, by being honest, I became aware of failings and my limitations. My course peers and trainers supported me, as we did each other, but I needed more.

A final consequence of personal counselling was the experience of this in itself. I found it traumatic, inspirational and a real indulgence. I appreciated and benefited hugely from experiencing the therapeutic relationship at first hand which, I can put hand on heart and say, was very influential on my subsequent work with clients. I had been through the process too.

Isla

In the first year of my course I went for counselling though I also had gone before the beginning of the course. On the course we had some peer counselling and some counselling exercises which often brought information to our conscious awareness. I am intending to work towards BAC Accreditation which currently requires 40 hours of personal therapy. I feel it is essential to have the experience of being a client, of being in that situation and realising what it is like to be there. In this way we can be more informed.

Chrissie

During my own counselling I struggled very hard with this aspect of counselling; I wanted someone to tell me how to be, to be accepted, as throughout my life I had been defined by how others wanted or expected me to be or, to be more accurate, how I perceived others' expectations of me. My counsellor gave me permission just to be me and it was one of the most terrifying and, at the same time, liberating experiences I have ever had. It was a leap into the unknown, a journey during which I was able to begin to find out who I really am. It is a journey that will take a lifetime to complete, since it did not end when my counselling ended but it did, as I have often found with others, begin on that first evening when my counselling began . . . when I was given permission to just be me.

Angie

Once I started my training I began to realise that my current counsellor did not listen enough to me. She was very morally supportive but she also gave me lots of unwanted advice and information until I felt I had no real autonomy in the relationship. She seemed like the 'expert' in our relationship; I felt frustrated because I felt unheard. I felt resentful because I was paying her to tell me my agenda. I felt angry because by now I believed I could do better. I also felt inadequate that once she had explained my 'problem' to me it did not 'go away' in one session. I also felt *politically incorrect* and blamed myself for not *feeling* politically correct (I knew all the words and ways I 'should' feel but *didn't* feel them). I am no longer with that original counsellor. However, I found the experience useful because with that therapist I started some of my most fundamental processing — the rebelling against some of my most deeply held constructs.

Looking back on that experience I can see that it was a useful lesson for me in how

I wanted to *be* in a counselling relationship. I was still in my second year of training when I moved on to another more person-centred counsellor. However, I could sense that even though my new counsellor was trying to be person-centred, I began to wonder if she was wanting to try Gestalt (her other qualification) on me. When I finally asked her, she confirmed my suspicion. I stayed with her for three years altogether before we both decided we had gone as far as we could in that relationship. I wanted only person-centred counselling. She felt she could not wholly give me that. The longer I was in training the more I wanted a *pure* person-centred experience.

Carol

It was the continuing search for my personal meanings with regard to my past and present experiences that led me eventually to seek individual counselling. I decided to make use of the college counselling service which was available free to students and to my knowledge then, open-ended. My experience of being a client in that setting for the four years that followed carried a mixture of significant gains and losses including some deeply-felt disappointments.

My therapy revealed a 'less than' person-centred relationship, though at the time was a very special relationship, which allowed me in its own way to concentrate on different aspects of myself that hindered my life and my process of training. It also revealed my personal reservations about placing rigid time limits and having numerous breaks as a contractual condition on the therapy. It seemed to me that my counselling at college put me through a number of trials through which I discovered my personal fears, anxieties, needs and expectations as a client. I also grew to understand more accurately my personal style as a developing counsellor and the terms on which I wish to offer counselling.

Perhaps, above all, my counselling experience uncovered my personal difficulty to follow the limits of what is acceptable and tolerable to me in a close and unequal relationship, which was one of many things which kept me entrenched in it for so long. A new world began to open for me when I gave myself the opportunity to re-engage in further counselling, this time with a therapist who was person-centred in a real sense.

During counselling training, I realised that I felt scared of the prospect of seeking out personal counselling. It seemed strange to me that I was in an area which I was reluctant to use myself. I did eventually work with a counsellor over a period of three months and later with another therapist for over nine months. My experience was positive and I was able to start to resolve issues which I had experienced for many years. It was not an easy process. It was scary and painful. At other times, I was reluctant to attend sessions and felt stuck and unable to move on.

Lucy

The most difficult feelings aroused were when I challenged myself to take action. I initially attempted to accept my feelings and learn to live openly with these feelings. However, it soon became apparent in the sessions that accepting my feelings was the first stage of healing for me. The next stage was to confront the people who were involved in how I was feeling. Taking this form of action was the most difficult part of the process for me. However, it proved to be incredibly rewarding and helpful in exorcising many of my fears.

points to ponder

Like any client in person-centred counselling, the number of sessions you have is ultimately up to you. The only 'rules' are for course or professional association requirements. Specific courses may require trainees to complete a set number of hours in personal therapy. It is important to check the criteria for each course, as they differ in their requirements. As for professional associations, the BAC currently requires counsellors who are applying for accreditation to have had at least 40 hours of personal counselling as part of their qualifying criteria (as of Sept 1999). The BAC Code of Ethics & Practice for Counsellors (under review) does not explicitly specify a need for personal counselling though it does highlight the need to 'maintain continuing professional development' (B.6.1.1. Jan 98) and is taken by some to imply personal counselling.

• Check whether personal counselling is a requirement of the course and, if so, clarify how many hours are expected. At the time of writing, there is a continuing debate about the need for a specific number of personal counselling sessions as a necessary part of training. On the one side it is argued that a counsellor cannot be effective unless they have experienced being a client and have used this to work on a major personal issue. On the other side, it is felt that this should only be a rule of thumb, may not be absolutely necessary for everyone, and can vastly increase the cost of counselling training.

• Even if you think you won't or don't need personal counselling, remember that it can be invaluable for you to know what the experience is like for your clients. Danny makes an interesting point here, 'How could I be with someone on a journey of understanding if I had not experienced that for myself?'.

• You are quite likely to want to have a period of personal counselling to work through some issues for which there may not be adequate course time or support. As Victoria points out, 'I decided about halfway through the second year to undertake personal counselling', and she goes on to explain why.

• For many people the number of sessions they have will be influenced significantly by the cost. Carol was lucky, 'I decided to make use of the college counselling service which was available free to students and, to my knowledge, open-ended'.

• Do you want to see a person-centred counsellor? If so, you will be able to note how they work and this might help in your professional development. You may also feel more at ease with the same approach in which you are training, thus allowing you to focus on your needs within the counselling relationship rather than on the approach.

• Choosing a counsellor from an alternative therapeutic approach may help you consolidate your likes and dislikes of the Person-Centred Approach. It allows you to experience an alternative approach as well as study it. It may help offer you a fresh insight into your current practice and approach. Each alternative approach views and works with the individual in a different way. Personal counselling from a non person-centred therapist may help you challenge and explore person-centred therapy further.

person-centred
counselling
training

**section
c**

**profes-
sional
develop-
ment**

The previous section on *personal* development represented only one part of the overall process of counselling training. The current section deals with the skills, acumen, experience and training which we will need to learn and practise to help us become counsellors and is referred to as *professional* development. We can be very astute, have a reasoned set of attitudes and values, and a very clear grasp of our self-awareness (including how we react and behave in response to any interaction or experience), but, without the skills of communication and counselling, we will not become proficient counsellors.

Becoming a counsellor is not just about having the right attitudes and good counselling skills either. We need to know how to work in the professional world of counselling alongside other professionals: teachers, social workers, doctors and nurses. Having confidence in your competence to do this will make you a credible professional and a well-rounded counsellor.

Although training will give us time for personal development, and practice to help us attain the necessary skills, counselling training is only the start of what will become, for many, a lifelong process. Just because we complete a training course, however good we may be, we do not leave knowing everything. Even after this period we will be influenced by our colleagues, further workshops and training, the development of the profession, the experience we build up from our client work and new insights from journals and books. We may, for instance, settle into a counselling job focusing on a particular group of clients, those suffering from substance abuse or a specific mental illness. We may choose to work in a particular environment — the commercial workplace, counselling education or primary care. These will all influence our way of working, our attitude to counselling and our enthusiasm, commitment and motivation.

Chapter 7 reveals that many trainees, even with the support and encouragement of course colleagues and staff, question whether they will *ever* feel they have the skills and confidence to become a counsellor. This is often a key part of the training, as we wrestle with new concepts and challenges. This chapter addresses the challenge which may well present itself frequently during training, 'will I *ever* become a competent counsellor?' The purpose of featuring this topic is because this question can be a real learning yardstick for trainees. Sometimes, the skills practice, the progress of peers, the client work and the feedback from staff can give a feeling that there is a long way to go to be proficient in the art of counselling. This may feel intimidating for some and for others this may be that useful checkpoint.

Chapter 8 then focuses on theory — a necessary component of counselling learning. Carl Rogers spent his whole life developing his theoretical constructs. We can benefit from this valuable archive of work to learn about this approach — why, when and how it works and also when it might not. While Carl Rogers is credited with being the architect of the Person-Centred Approach, much of value has been developed by others, both during his life and since his death. This counselling approach affords a continual opportunity for development, refinement and fine-tuning. The principles will remain, but current and future research will generate new paths and insights and will filter into the training process through practice.

Chapter 9 offers us an insight into the experience of practising counselling skills on the course. Often, practice development is done in small groups where trainees take turns to practise being a client and a counsellor so they can practise the skills. It is through practice that we learn, not only competence but also confidence. This gives us the chance to give, to receive and to observe. Much of the early fear for trainees is trying to remember what to say, but the essence of counselling is the absence of planning, the presence of openness and spontaneity which facilitate the honest and real therapeutic relationship.

Professional-level training requires trainees to see *real* clients during their training, just like doctors-in-training in their final years treat real patients.

Then Chapter 10 records what it was like for some trainees working with the first *real* clients and the excitement and dramas of working on a counselling placement. As trainees started working with their first clients, they realised their apprehension and concern about skills practice could pale into significance when dealing with real clients! The sobering reality of the first client can be tempered by the faith and conviction that previous skills practice existed for this very reason.

Professional counsellors are required to have their work supervised by an independent person. The purpose is to ensure that the counsellor is practising as ethically and effectively as possible.

Chapter 11 concludes this section by reflecting on the importance and value of the supervision of our work. As well as acting as a means to monitor our work, supervision can become a key learning resource. The concept of supervision, in its many guises, will, in a limited way, be illustrated in this chapter. Some recommendations are offered to help choose a suitable individual supervisor — the individuals who will closely monitor the progress and development of counsellors, from trainee status and beyond.

7

can I become a competent counsel-lor?

You may be wondering whether you are made of the right stuff to be a counsellor. Identifying your personal expectations is one step towards helping you to assess your potential. What are your expectations of yourself as a counsellor? Do you expect to be competent or incompetent, satisfactory or a shining beacon of excellence? Will you experience the work as difficult, easy, traumatic, challenging? Do you expect to need or want further training, post qualification? Will you need to be supervised in your work? Will you need personal counselling?

Understanding what *competence* means for you will assist you in forming realistic expectations of yourself. When Laura first came across the term *competent counsellor* or *good enough counsellor*, she was surprised. It challenged her values. She was brought up to feel that you are either 'good' or 'bad' at things but not *competent*. (Actually, at first she wondered if it was another piece of counselling jargon for people to use in a politically correct fashion.) But she now understands this phrase more in relation to herself. Laura thinks that it offers her a realistic and compassionate way of viewing herself.

When Laura realised that her way of viewing her skills and abilities was as either 'good' or 'bad', it explained many things to her such as her approach to new skills and interests. She would throw herself into learning a new skill but would never reach the magical point of being *good* — there was always something she could see that needed improving. The term 'good enough' gave her the freedom to give up the chase for perfection. She now understands that her expectations of herself were too high — these expectations were encouraging her to set goals and judge herself and this was impacting upon her natural desire to learn and have fun while learning. She can recognise now that her approach to learning grew from her family background where there was constant encouragement to strive to do better and achieve more — she was not giving herself credit for what she had achieved and continued to bully herself into trying to do better. (If Laura took this approach into a counselling relationship, she would be offering her client a therapist who was unable, in part, to value herself. If Laura was not valuing herself, would she be fully able to value the client?)

So, the expectations you hold will impact on your client work and personal development during training. Training can offer an opportunity to explore your expectations and begin to understand were they come from and it may help you recognise whether your personal expectations are impinging on your relationship with your client — and your training peers can assist you to explore this area.

For Rick, the stage of being a competent counsellor came after training, facilitated, in the main, by his counselling supervisor. He'd had the same supervisor right from the start and this gave him the benefit of having someone watch his progress. Much of his training had been geared to learning what to do and what not to do. There was inherent flexibility, but the message was to 'toe the line'. He felt he had to follow the Person-Centred Approach as it stood. But it took him some time to realise that he had allowed himself to be restricted by the impression that he had to follow a fairly rigid doctrine. As his client experience blossomed he learned that what was important was to find his own interpretation of this approach, but based on his training and on his understanding of the philosophy. He concluded that Carl Rogers was proposing a *way of being* both as a client *and* counsellor. It was up to Rick, with his supervisor, to learn what the Person-Centred Approach was actually about for him through practice. He has developed into a person-centred counsellor but it has taken several years to reach this stage. The end of a Diploma course in person-centred counselling, for Rick, was not the making of such a counsellor but the road to becoming one.

Jenny

I feel I am becoming a more contented and confident person, although I have been through doubtful times as to my suitability to be a counsellor and sometimes the length of the process seems overwhelming. However, I have a kind of hope that if I have come so far in the first half of the course that, by the end, I will have achieved more self-awareness. I still feel there are blanks in me that I know little about and that these interfere with me relating to clients.

Michael

I remember I often questioned whether I could ever become a competent counsellor. Frequently I wrestled with the core issues of the Person-Centred Approach; I had many questions and there seemed so few answers. I just couldn't get the hang of it to start with. My questioning, disbelieving and sceptical approach led me to consider why this was happening. In some ways I was testing the process and myself. I also became aware of a block which was getting in the way. I was confused about how counsellors *should be*, that is, how should we behave? It seemed I was trying to emulate the core conditions and integrate this into who I was as a person.

It took me time, and many debates with peers and tutors, to come to my conclusion that I could chose to apply such conditions to my way of being when I wanted to, when it suited me. I don't have to be congruent and transparent with someone outwith a counselling relationship if I don't want to. I can be judgemental if I want to be. But what allows me this freedom is the choice to be whatever I want to be in my own life. However, by observing peers, sometimes I would notice a particular attitude or approach that I may have disagreed with and, while I am happy to accept this disagreement, I sometimes wondered how this attitude or approach impacted on their counselling work

For instance, if I noticed someone on my course who was a real 'loudmouth', always taking the spotlight during workshops or discussions, I would wonder whether this would affect how they worked with clients. What power dynamics would pervade? Not only did I learn to challenge such attitudes to encourage the person to reflect on this behaviour but it made me consider how I am outwith the counselling arena and what attitudes or behaviours I exhibit and how does this impact on my counselling work. Awareness and a willingness to challenge oneself is, I think, the key.

After all the doubt, I now believe in my abilities as a counsellor, I trust and have faith in the approach but equally I am happy to observe the limitations too, both mine and that of the approach. That's OK.

Vera

I experienced the first two terms of the Diploma as quite de-skilling and although it provided vocabulary for what I had already been doing, the analysing of my work led me to question whether I was doing it 'right', whether I was understanding it fully and even if I was suitable to be a counsellor. I felt a lot of anxiety towards the end of the first year because we had to do a three-hour exam on what we had learnt during the year. This threw me back to my experience of school, exams and being tested which had felt pressurised and frightening.

Iain

I have been definitely 'stuck' at times. This is why I feel it is important to have a good support network but it can be difficult to find this outside the group and non-counselling people do not understand what is going on. Having said this, it was also difficult to seek the support from my counselling group too.

At certain 'stuck' periods I was left with some pretty defensive thinking that I was not 'good enough'. Furthermore, I would sometimes consider that counselling was 'dodgy'. Equally so, I sometimes felt that my tutor was a 'con man'.

Latticia

Before starting my counselling training I had no doubts about my ability to become a competent counsellor. A couple of months into training I experienced chronic doubts concerned with the possibility that I might soon be calling myself a counsellor. Subconsciously, I think I assumed that I would be taught how to counsel. It came as a surprise to find myself doubting my abilities. In fact, my doubts were also insidiously making inroads into my view of myself as a professional working with people with mental health problems. And this was my post prior to starting the counselling course.

It seemed that I was in the process of questioning both my way of working and my personal philosophy. As a result of this, I felt stranded. I had given up my 'professional' status in order to explore my philosophy and to check out whether the Person-Centred Approach was right for me. For a while this left me adrift. But I think it was worth it. The process helped me question my working practice with people experiencing mental health problems. It helped me challenge a role which I had developed where I was trying to find the answers for the client. Through my training I experienced an increase in my ability to 'stay with the client' which seems to help the client explore their issues at their own pace.

Liz

I still question whether I'm a competent counsellor, so nothing has changed. I actually like this, it's a sort of checking process for me. There are times when I really know that the counselling I have offered a client has been very successful. Not only do I hear them thank me, perhaps with a card, but I can resonate with the belief from them. Other times, particularly with clients who I only see once, I question how effective I have been for them. I also question whether counselling *per se* has been of use to them. In many of these cases I will never know and I am able to live with this uncertainty.

points to ponder

- You may frequently question whether you are good enough to become a counsellor. There is no such thing as a perfect counsellor, only a proficient and experienced one. You can become this with supervised practice and experience.

- You may question the validity and usefulness of the Person-Centred Approach. It is a difficult set of concepts to grasp, not just with regard to the academic or theoretical aspects but especially in understanding how to provide the core conditions of empathy, unconditional positive regard and congruence.

- It is hard work training as a counsellor, much harder than most people often imagine. There will be times when you want to give up. And this may be the right decision to make. Vera claims her first two terms were 'quite de-skilling' and that the end-of-year exam provoked 'anxiety', evoking past 'frightening' feelings about school exams.

- The support of your peers and course staff can be invaluable and, as Iain pointed out, having 'a good support network' is important. But he found outside the group 'people do not understand what is going on' and in the group 'it was difficult to seek . . . support'.

- A word which Iain uses a couple of times is 'stuck'. This term is frequently quoted by trainees to describe the static feeling they may feel about their progress.

- Where do intuitions, gut feelings or hunches fit in? What do you make of your own sense of intuition? Are there times when your intuition is more accurate than other times? Is there the risk that our intuition can be restricted by having tunnel vision?

- Appreciate compliments when you get them. Liz speaks of how she gets her thanks from a sort of 'resonance'.

- Depending on the counselling context within which you may work, there may be a tendency for a large proportion of clients to turn up for only one appointment and not return. How will this affect you in the sense of not knowing why they do not return?

8
theory

The Person-Centred Approach does have a substantial theory behind it. Carl Rogers wrote his first major book describing the beginnings of his new approach in 1942, and in 1951 wrote *Client-Centered Therapy,* in which he outlined his theory of personality. In 1957 he described the therapeutic conditions which we have, in this book, called the *core conditions.* Since then, Rogers wrote many more books and there have been thousands of books, chapters and research papers devoted to the development of client-centred and person-centred theory.

As each year goes by, more of this work becomes available in the United Kingdom. However, since most readers of this book are at the very beginning of their learning about counselling and person-centred theory, we have suggested some simple starting points for reading in Appendix 2.

The purpose of this chapter is to illustrate the impact that theory has on counselling training. In this book we are not going to try to describe the underlying theoretical concepts. We would not do justice to person-centred theory if we were to attempt such a simple summary. A reader interested in developing a better understanding would be advised to refer to the book list in Appendix 6 and maybe even to consult the authoritative works of Carl Rogers.

Is it necessary to understand the theoretical perspective of the Person-Centred Approach in order to practise counselling? The answer has to be 'Yes!' It provides us with the foundation to become proficient and competent counsellors. It can give the counsellor a firm foothold from which they can develop their own ideas about counselling. In addition, it can assist the counsellor in times when he/she feels they are losing their client or are unable to understand the process the client is going through. The counsellor can return to the theory and attempt to understand their practice in light of the theoretical framework.

A theory creates a common language through which counsellors can discuss their ideas. This language affords active use of particular vocabulary such as *acceptance, empathy, genuineness, active listening, reflecting* etc. These terms suggest a certain way of being. Indeed the name of the approach itself instantly shows that the person, the human individual, is at the centre of the approach. Our use and understanding of language can have a profound impact upon our thinking, feelings and actions. An understanding of theory gives us access to a rich language and meaning from which our ideas can be developed.

A theoretical framework also offers a clear starting point for research. It enables the researcher to develop his/her ideas within a framework. It provides a baseline from which the researcher can attempt to add new dimensions or challenge current thoughts.

On the other hand, some people believe that theory can foster a rigid way of working and creates a counsellor who adheres to an inflexible rule book. The other side to strictly adhering to a theoretical approach is the potential loss of individuality. There is a risk that the counsellor develops a set of *rigid rules* from the approach rather than a *flexible framework.* The counsellor may become over-dependent upon the approach and not listen to their own developing ideas which could be potentially moulded into their individual style. In addition, and some would say worst of all, there is the risk that the counsellor ignores what is coming from his/her client because it does not fit into the counsellor's theoretical framework.

The counsellor may experience difficulty in challenging the approach. This can be a risk in training where the trainee is absorbing a wide range of information and views, much of which may be new. Although training is an ideal forum in which to challenge and test out opinions and views, it can also be a difficult time to do this. The trainee is attempting to assimilate large amounts of information and integrate their feelings in relation to the material and it can be overwhelming and difficult to find words to convey incubating thoughts and feelings. Despite the difficulty of this process, the trainee can experience a great sense of achievement from this struggle. During this process the trainee will have managed to integrate their thoughts, experiences and feelings within the theoretical framework. It is through this process that the theory becomes a living approach integrated into the counsellor's life. When this happens we can say that the individual is living in a person-centred way rather than just 'wearing' the views and theory like a coat.

The importance of theory was a difficult question for Laura to address. She found it confusing because when she looked at her significant learning, it appeared to stem from experience and not from theory. However, reflecting on this, she realised that much of her past experience had been underpinned by theoretical concepts. She had integrated the theory to the extent that it *felt* as though it had always been a part of her. The essence of theory to Laura is to use the aspects of it which relate to current experience and not to attempt to mould one's experience into a particular theory. When Laura meets an experience which appears inexplicable, she can return to theory as a source of further enlightenment, in the same way that she can discuss the issue within counselling supervision, with a friend or with her partner.

Rick found theory at times both a great help and a great hindrance. It took him some time to realise that what was important was not just to learn about theoretical issues 'parrot fashion' but more to integrate this into who we are and how we practice as counsellors. Much of the theory seeks to validate, authenticate and evaluate the process of person-centred counselling. What seemed useful for Rick was to have a sound knowledge of this process but then to focus on particular aspects which felt relevant and of interest to him.

Many of the case-studies featured respond to the request for contributions by focusing on an *academic* perspective. Theory is often seen as the academic or 'intellectual' side of counselling training and with this perception it can appear off-putting for some people. Many of us will not be used to reading textbooks and writing essays and this can be difficult to get back into. Above all, theory exists to help us in our understanding.

It is usually not necessary to have a qualification in psychology or social sciences before starting a person-centred counselling course, although it may help to have some understanding of psychological approaches.

Don't worry if you have not studies for many years, you will almost certainly not be alone, as you will see from the testimonies on the following pages. Your tutors should give you plenty of help and support when it comes to understanding theory.

If you are worried about how you will get on with the theory, start off with a simple introductory book then graduate to something written by Carl Rogers.

I had never been a big reader but now I found myself reading material I could not   *Donald*
put down; each page provoked an internal experience which provoked another. I
was never alone, I always had me and, thankfully, still do have now.

      Irene   I think, here, I need to say something about the purely academic strain in training.
That in the two years that were so amazingly, life-givingly rich and vital there was
no shirking, no retreat from the thought process. The intricacies of making the
attempt for philosophical consistency and integrity, to turn philosophy into praxis
by skills.

The hours we spent striving through taped practice to turn the words and the
practice sessions into something real, alive, comprehended and applicable outside
the course was as crucial as all the self-awareness work. Without the two strands
in tension and in alliance, the struggle to become alive would have been vitiated
and death-giving.

For me I found theory or the academic side was more explicit at the start of the   *Iain*
course but then it became more subtle as the course progressed.

My course was person-centred and psychodynamic and with this mix I had no
difficulties with any of the theoretical concepts from an academic point of view.
Assimilating the concepts into my experience does take time. In some cases it
took a long time to understand what is happening in the approach process but this
can sometimes be explained in or by a particular theoretical perspective.

      Clare   The theory part of one of my modules in combination with my experiences in the
development group, the skills practice, the residential as well as the self-focusing
hand-outs, tutorials, written work and my work with clients, moved me greatly
into developing my capacity to become aware of my feelings and be more open
and responsive to my experiencing of others. For example, listening to other
people's experiences in the development group put me deeply in touch with my
feelings regarding several of my experiences. I became aware of the fact that I
limited aspects of myself by feeling threatened with material long denied to my
awareness and by letting (the significant) others introject their judgements upon
me on certain issues.

In my effort to understand different ways of thinking about therapy, I focused on
extensive personal reading and reflection which enabled me to clarify several
theoretical concepts as well as my own understanding. It was my preference to
choose essay titles related to Rogers' work. For example, during the first term, I gave
myself the opportunity to explore the concept of subjectivity — what I saw as the
leading and essential element of the person-centred concept — and its place in the
fields of phenomenology, existentialism, philosophy and psychology. This unveiled
my natural eagerness to liberate my subjective world of knowing, to recognise myself
as an individual in my own right, to get down to the real unique me.

I found out how my own therapeutic experiences proved, for me, the connections   *Annie*
between philosophy, theory and practice. My experience of the practice proved

the theory which in turn validated the person-centred philosophy. That experience, and the wonderful memories I have of them, help to keep me on my track. I never tire of the excitement I feel when the point is proven once again with each new client, each time we meet.

Ronnie The theory on the course, for me, became the battleground of debate, argument and questioning. I enjoyed writing one assignment on 'congruence' but I found there were so many inherent contradictions within the core conditions when you really pick at them. But I found that this is more so if you are adhering to a strictly theoretical debate. The gist of counselling is based on theory, but it is the application and the human relating which to some extent defies theory in its pure, limiting sense.

I wrote another assignment on Rogers' 'Theory of Personality'. While this was fascinating in its own right, my overriding question was Rogers' motivation for developing such a theory. I thought the Person-Centred Approach was about being accepting and non-judgemental, specifically not to label and stereotype our clients but to take them as they are, wherever they are. Surely this theory is stereotyping and labelling? My answer was to use this theory as a means to understand the human condition, strictly for learning, and not let any judgement interfere with my client work.

I suppose in retrospect this did help me to appreciate the clients I could work with and those I could not, due to their state, or readiness for counselling or my skills to be available and proficient for them.'

The 19 Propositions and Rogers' Theory of Personality which were presented in the first term have only really just started making sense as I complete my assignment on the theory. I am still not really seeing how the theory applies to clients, although this is coming out more in supervision groups and I think I need more experience to see the whole picture better. *Julia*

Sam I found theory to be very useful but before this made sense to me it bored the hell out of me. It took me ages to see any relevance. To be honest, I'm still a bit sceptical about things I was 'taught'. Yes, I learned to be a counsellor but much of the theory was left in the classroom. There was no real connection to the real world. I meet up with a few of my former classmates now and again and we all feel that much of the theory seems irrelevant to our work.

I liked how we were taught the theoretical side of person-centred counselling. I suppose individually we took out of this what was important for us. For instance, I was fascinated by two main areas, firstly, the theory behind the therapeutic process, as devised by Rogers and, secondly, personality theory. For me both underpin everything in my counselling work. For the therapeutic process I retain an awareness of progress and sometimes when I feel things are not moving forward I can check this out. Personality theory helps me to measure how people are in counselling. I don't actually diagnose or stereotype but it seems to help me in some way. However, there were other aspects which went over my head, such as psychopathology. *Juliet*

Gillian   I'm glad I had the opportunity to comment on 'theory'. Since completing my training some five years ago, I have been progressively aware about how impractical the theory can be in the reality of a counselling environment. I feel that the structures imposed by 'learning the theory' actually typecast me in a counselling style that was not me and was not appropriate. It has taken me many years to learn the experience of counselling and in some ways this has been by shedding the theory. I know we need to start with a base, a foundation of knowledge, and I don't argue against this, but I do feel quite strongly about the tight channel that we seem to swim in order to get our Diplomas or whatever. The whole point about person-centred therapy is surely to dispense with structure and to counsel in a 'person-centred' way?

I thought that person-centred therapy was all about being experiential. I had hoped there would be no theoretical input but I was wrong. My Diploma course was much more academic than I expected. This hindered me because I frequently got panicky about not being able to grasp the academic side.   *Gaby*

points to ponder

- Person-centred theory can, for some, be difficult to grasp. It may also be confusing at times, yet at other times seem quite familiar to you and easy to understand. It may be that your approach to working with people is naturally 'person-centred' and discovering the theory offers you a working framework from which to develop further. Donald gives us a good example of someone who became excited by this new work, 'I had never been a big reader but now I found myself reading material I could not put down; each page provoked an internal experience which provoked another'.

- You may find that understanding the theory can substantially help in your personal *and* professional development.

- The theoretical aspects of counselling are a necessary part of the training. The theory can assist you in challenging your attitudes and those of others. It can offer a stimulating arena in which to explore your values and beliefs.

- Course staff should be happy to help you through the maze of theoretical understanding. Theory exists to help in our understanding and learning. If there is a block somewhere it might be useful to consider why this may exist.

- A trainee may experience conflict, a tension or a struggle when challenging theory. Feelings of conflict may come from self, peers and course tutors as a response to your challenge. This may be an interesting area to explore. You may become aware of reacting to an individual as an authority figure or feeling the need of a definitive guide or set of rules. You may also become aware of the value of challenging theory and the level of development and maturity of your ideas, as a result.

• If you just cannot relate to the theory, ask a course staff member to illustrate some element of theory by way of demonstration or real-life example. For example, in Chapter 4, Cynthia speaks of her struggle in accepting herself. She says, 'In Rogers' terms, I am developing a strong internal locus of evaluation, and in my own words, I am doing the harvesting of the last six years — I am becoming more and more my own person'.

• The understanding of theory as a mechanism to fuel ideas and learning can be enriching. Ronnie found that this 'became a battleground of debate, argument and questioning'.

The reference to 'locus of evaluation' refers to the 'place of evaluating'. For instance, someone who speaks of an 'internal locus of evaluation' will be referring to how they trust the feelings they are experiencing in relation to themselves and others. This results in the individual feeling more actively confident in their response to themselves and others. An 'external locus of evaluation' refers to an individual relying more on sources outside themselves, i.e. parents, employers or peer groups. Most of us live by a set of 'rules' which are imposed on us by society, government and organisations — the cultures of which we choose to be a part. We each make decisions about which rules we break or ignore and those we uphold.

9
develop-
ing
person-
centred
practice

In person-centred training, the trainers try to create a forum where trainees can essentially refine their understanding, experiencing and communication of the core conditions: congruence, empathy and unconditional positive regard. This involves, for instance, *role-play* (offering a 'pretend' client these core conditions) or sometimes having trainees counselling each other as 'real' clients.

It is probably useful to highlight here, the three types of counselling 'practice' on training courses:
1. 'Role-play' when someone pretends to be someone they are not or pretends to have a problem they do not.
2. Where two trainees agree to do *co-learner counselling*. One person is the counsellor and the other is the client — they remain themselves and talk about their own real-life issues, but both acknowledge that the prime aim of the session is learning, not counselling.
3. Bona fide real counselling with real clients. Such sessions are usually tape-recorded for evaluation and reviewed by tutors, peers and/or supervisors.

There are different views as to the value of course-based skills practice in the form of role-plays or co-learner counselling. It is suggested by some trainers that the process is artificial and therefore not representative of a real experience.

In its favour, course-based skills development can offer a safe environment in which to experiment with your counselling practice. It allows the trainee to record their practice perhaps via video and/or audio recording equipment which when replayed can offer a great deal of food for thought — allowing the trainee to study their practice in minute detail. As well as this, the trainee can benefit from valuable feedback from their peers. The trainee in practice-counsellor role often has the benefit of feedback from observers such as course staff and fellow trainees. The trainee acting as client can also offer the trainee counsellor valuable insight into how it feels to be counselled. As an observer they can learn how to evaluate someone else's work.

It can be challenging and stimulating putting into action what you have been discussing in training. It is a good opportunity to practise describing to a client what person-centred counselling is and any specific information that they might find useful, such as defining a counselling contract, describing limits of time, supervision, cancellations, costs etc.

As a client, Laura experienced co-learner counselling as a positive and often productive experience. She would choose an issue which she could explore in a time-limited way. It was often invaluable working with a variety of individuals at depth.

Often skills practice yields positive and productive experiences for individuals, but this is not to say that it can be an intimidating proposition for the trainee. It may feel artificial and personally exposing and each of these feelings can be experienced by both the client and the counsellor. Receiving and offering feedback is a crucial aspect of skills practice but it can feel very destructive if feedback is offered in a particularly negative way.

Laura found it difficult on one occasion when she was given some feedback in a negative and critical manner. However, the learning she gained from the experience was immense. It focused her attention on offering feedback in an appropriate way and at a pace which the individual can hear and take on board receptively. Your feedback will be wasted if you offer it in such a way that it cannot be heard.

Course-based skills practice can seem very daunting in the beginning — there is a lot happening all at once. 'Pretend' counsellors are aware of a video camera or cassette recorder *and* an observer *and* also perhaps a trainer. It may be difficult *not* to feel self-conscious but most trainees will point out that this concern will soon recede with experience and practice.

Rick remembers being particularly anxious during one of his first skills practice experiences on a Certificate Course in Counselling Skills. As a 'pretend' counsellor, not only did he momentarily forget what to say or do but at that time, if asked, he would not have been able to remember his own name! He did find the experience very daunting at first, feeling so self-conscious. Not only did a video-playback highlight his counselling responses but he was further reminded of his receding hairline! (Rick allegedly changed his hairstyle during subsequent counselling training!)

What really helped Rick was to get a couple of friends and head off to a room during a lunch-hour with the video camera, where they could practise without getting anxious about others watching. They did have some of these sessions replayed to supervision groups so all could listen, watch, applaud or criticise as was seen fit. He found that things improved with repeated practice.

Above all, skills practice is as the term implies — the practice of our skills. If we can assume we *will* make mistakes then the learning derived from the experience will help us improve and become more confident and competent.

Many courses use a 'triad' format for skills practice. This means three trainees will each take a particular role — Client, Counsellor and Observer. Over an assigned period of time a role-play will be carried out, usually on a topic chosen by the 'pretend' client. The job of the Observer is to watch, listen and note the Counsellor and to feedback observations, habits, mannerisms and any useful insight. This observing role is obviously very useful for the Counsellor but also the Observer can really learn how to feedback constructively.

Many courses also make extensive use of video and audiotaping of the role-plays or co-learner counselling sessions.

This was only a twenty-week course and for the first ten weeks the practical skills training section was a mess. I learnt nothing much about counselling as personalities got in the way of any real constructive work and practice.

Dan

> *Jenny*
>
> Skills practice groups were sensitively handled, although the quality of equipment left a lot to be desired. Audio/videotaping sessions which then proved to be inaudible when played back to the supervision group was demotivating and frustrating. Despite this, feedback was constructive and easy to digest and my group was very supportive.

Despite having been through the video process in my counselling skills course, I found the Diploma sessions quite tense. I feel it was because we had all seemingly reached a set standard of skills proficiency yet the video playback of our work shocked us all. I remember blushing as I watched my posture. My head seemed to stay at an uncomfortable angle and it went up and down continuously like one of those nodding-dog toys you see in the back of cars! What was breakneck, however, was the speed of learning. Our supportive, yet, I felt, rather overtly confrontational, tutor continually asked us why we said this or what was going on for us when we said that.

Ron

It was like a round of golf, at least at my dubious standard. One video would seem almost perfect, spot on target, but then the very next one might be a complete duff one, where I missed every cue, all suitable reflection and seemed completely out of touch. These up-and-down days were very stressful as we each became our own worst judge and executioner.

> *Issie*
>
> There was no video work apart from one session in the first year and this made me aware of how I looked but I'm not sure how useful any further work would be. I did find, however, that an essential quality of the interaction between practice counsellor and practice client is lost when viewing the video. It is second-hand, where you are not 'in' the experience of relating and it could be rather superficial dealing with body-language points. It could be useful if the person videoed could relate the experience to the observed body language or tone of voice.

The lowest points of the course for me were often in our Skills Group, e.g. we were meant to do an exercise in which we tried to look at ourselves from the client's perspective — how they saw us. I found this, at the time, impossible to visualise and became very upset. I talked it through with one of my friends on the course and came to the conclusion that this was part of my legacy as an only child with no siblings and no means of seeing/experiencing how another person saw me.

Veronique

I found the video work on the course quite frightening but very helpful. It was an opportunity for much deeper exploration and analysis of my work.

> *Anne-Marie*
>
> Our practice during training was in triads; three people working together as client, counsellor and observer. The observer's role was to give feedback to the counsellor on aspects of their way of being with the client, i.e. what helped the client stay with his/her process, move forward or held them back. We rotated roles within an

approximately 90-minute session to enable each trainee to experience every role. We usually allowed a ten-minute feedback time for each rotation. Occasionally a tutor would sit in on part of the 90-minute session. We asked tutors to observe particular aspects of our practice — for example, how congruent or empathic we were.

In triad sessions I would usually work with new people in each module so as to gain as much variety of experience as possible. Sometimes I worked with people with whom I felt safe enough to talk about problems I was having with peers, the course or some recent personal crisis. At the time I worried that this might be a cop-out. I realised, however, that I had the right to approach my process in my own way at my own pace. Getting the support I needed at the time was my way of self-caring and I was right to do that.

I had a mixed experience of working in triads, however. On a number of occasions I felt it was like the blind leading the blind. I did not feel confident about the understanding of some of my peers and not confident (or congruent) enough to point this out. I found client feedback more useful because the client had *experienced* me as a counsellor. However, I experienced some clients as reluctant to give me *negative* feedback even though this would have been the most useful feedback at the time. Mistakes are what I seem to learn from most, as well as, of course, feedback on what I did right. Tutors positively encouraged and even instructed all trainees to give each other positive *and* negative feedback.

A reluctance to give negative feedback became apparent as a group norm. When this aspect of our way of relating to each other came up, we discovered that connotations around the word 'negative' were giving rise to perceptions about being 'mean' or 'unkind'. We were rescuing each other from the pain of hearing unpleasantness about our practice. This reluctance was extremely unhelpful for me *and* I was also guilty of rescuing like this on numerous occasions.

I have other feelings about triad work that was based on the unnaturalness of the context. I never work with a third person in the room when I am counselling outside a training context. I was experiencing myself differently in triads to the way I experienced myself as both a counsellor and a client when there were just two of us in a room. In the latter situation I felt more congruent, my body was more relaxed. When I was working in triads, I was tense for the first ten minutes or so. Having said all that, I can see that if I could learn to really counsel in triads I could counsel even better with fewer distractions in the privacy of my more usual counselling settings.

Clare

Feedback during counselling-skills training led to a significant change in my way of working. The comments from a tutor who observed me during a practice session encouraged me to acknowledge my intuitive abilities. Before this I had been trying to work as a 'person-centred therapist'. But I was denying a part of myself. This feedback came at the right moment. I was feeling around in the dark during practice sessions. Sometimes it worked, sometimes it didn't. Acknowledging my intuition allowed me to start to really use myself within the counselling relationship. I instantly saw a difference in the process. I started to trust my sensing towards what the client was saying and check it out with him/her. During skills training and feedback I realised how important my intuition is to me and to my relationships with others. By trying to put it to one side I was denying a fundamental part of me — to the client and to me.

Tony   The most challenging part of the course was the video and reflection on sessions with peers and the submission of a video session with a volunteer client as part of the final assessment. There was also a significant level of skill enhancement and challenge which naturally led to deeper issues of which the skill was an indicator. The peer assessment sessions were challenging, supportive, enlightening and conducive to personal growth. From the feedback of others I think our peer support/ home group worked particularly well.

points to ponder

- You may experience many different emotions during skills practice. It can be difficult, exciting, painful, stimulating, fun and much more — it can be a valuable learning forum.

- You are likely to be recorded on video and/or audiotape which will probably be played back to your skills practice group. You may have good practice sessions and bad ones. As Ron explained, ' . . . one video would seem almost perfect, spot on target, but then the next one might be a complete duff one'.

- To prepare you for this perhaps you can try a practice development session at home with a friend or colleague and tape this. Listen to yourself and get used to hearing what you sound like.

- Everybody makes mistakes in practice development sessions. This can be invaluable for counselling learning. Don't be put off by 'silly' things you say or do. There is no such thing as a perfect session with real client work — we would all respond slightly differently, notice specific words or mannerisms and phrase our contributions differently.

- How we respond with feedback to our peers can be a crucial part of learning both for us and the rest of the group. Jenny found that 'feedback was constructive and easy to digest and [her] group was very supportive'. However, for Dan 'personalities got in the way of any real constructive work and practice'.

- Clarify the arrangement on confidentiality within practice development groups, noting whether colleagues (or staff) from other groups may be permitted to see/hear your tape. This is particularly relevant if your 'client' doesn't want anyone to see/hear the content and if an issue affects another member of the course. For example, your 'client' may be discussing a problem or issue which they may be experiencing with another course member. It is important that the client can retain control over their material. It is the counsellor's responsibility to bring clarity to this area.

- If you are expected to buy your own dictaphone or tape recorder to tape clients, remember to get equipment which is fairly unobtrusive in the counselling room, and a standard tape machine rather than spending quite a lot on an expensive tape recorder. Also, consider a loan of a tape recorder from a friend or relative or even a trainee from the previous year to save you buying one.

Do talk to past trainees and present colleagues about which equipment works best, and ask tutors for advice before committing to expensive equipment. Find out, for example, what equipment your training course uses so that you can make a compatible purchase.

You will probably find that your own voice is an important factor here. It is a good idea to visit a specialist local shop where you can try out different makes.

10 work experi- ence, place- ments and the first clients

You can find information on the range of settings in which counselling is practiced in BAC leaflets. Also, Tony Merry devotes pages 120–125 of *Learning and Being in Person-Centre d Counselling* to the training placement. Finally, Pete Sanders looks at a range of settings in which counselling is practised in *First Steps in Counselling,* pages107–112.

Work experience and placements are an integral part of counsellor training. Generally, courses will expect you to organise this area yourself. It can be a good idea to consider the options available before you start training. Is there a specific field of counselling in which you are interested? What are the reasons for your interest? Do you wish to develop a current area of work or are you looking to explore a new avenue?

You may be using your current workplace as work experience and intending to integrate your training and work. It may be an ideal time for you to develop your current working practice, building in the person-centred philosophy. This can prove a challenging experience, especially if there is conflict between your existing practice and the Person-Centred Approach — it is likely to require a great deal of discussion and exploration. However, you may discover that your workplace and the approach *are* compatible and comfortably allows for development of your practice. Alternatively, you may be interested in exploring an area of interest in which you have little experience.

There is a wide range of contexts within which counselling can be offered — in primary care, in colleges and universities, in the workplace, in the voluntary sector, custodial settings, self-help groups and mental health organisations and others. Each sector may involve a different way of working and will obviously feature a specific range of clients and presenting issues. The process of consideration of which client group suits you can be very insightful. Not only may this enable you to focus on a preferred group but also you may consider why a particular group or context is *not* suitable for you and could highlight personal development issues which could be important for you to explore.

Finding the appropriate placement is hard work requiring a high degree of commitment and a lot of investigation. It is helpful to understand the philosophy of the organisation with which you are hoping to work. It could prove problematic if you accept clients for counselling and then discover that you disagree with the organisational philosophy, e.g. policies and procedures relating to areas such as referral process, confidentiality, keeping records, supervision, time limit, requirements to give advice and information etc.

There may also be certain presenting issues which might either conflict with or challenge your own values, beliefs and morals or that you simply feel uncomfortable working with, e.g. child abuse, self-harm, substance use, gender issues, sexual orientation etc. At the same time it will be useful to consider why these difficulties exist and what makes you uncomfortable.

Your course may require you to do a set number of client hours (where you, the trainee counsellor, see clients) as part of the training. You may feel it necessary to clarify the potential number of clients your placement is able to refer. It may be that you are required to work with more than one organisation in order to meet your client hours, which can have the positive effect of increasing the breadth of your experience. However, this may also require you to adapt to different organisational management and policies.

Laura's first formal counselling during training placement was memorable. She felt nervous, very conscious of herself, the room and the seating arrangements — in fact, conscious of everything *except* the client. In preparing for this session Laura read the referral letter and promptly forgot the details but continued to worry about this during the session. As a result of her attention focused on these details, Laura was not 'with' her client. Not surprisingly, the client did not return for a second appointment. As a result of this experience, she chose not to read referral letters prior to seeing the client, rather she looked to the client to explain in their own way why they had come for counselling. Laura also took five to ten minutes prior to the session to be alone to focus on how she was feeling at that moment. This helped her to recognise if there were any residual feelings or issues around for her which might have interfered with her ability to attend to the client.

Rick felt very prepared for his first client. He had exhaustively practised his skills and considered a range of scenarios in advance. But he was not prepared to have as his first client . . . a counsellor! Immediately, he was hit with a fear of appearing incompetent or being evaluated and judged on the basis of his counselling experience. However, the first session was used to address this concern and this became one of Rick's most satisfying and rewarding counselling experiences. The big lesson learnt was that it is impossible to be totally prepared. In fact, part of the challenge and enthusiasm Rick feels now is *not* knowing what to expect, to be open to whatever and whoever comes to him.

It is almost inconceivable that anyone should attend a training course that does not include a substantial amount of work experience.

The British Association for Counselling has a scheme whereby it accredits courses that meet certain criteria. Courses apply and go through a rigorous process of scrutiny. Several of the many criteria involve work experience — in order to be accredited the course must require students to complete a *minimum* of 100 hours of actual client work. This means 100 hours of counselling with real clients, not just being at the doctor's surgery or college counselling service.

More can be found on accreditation of courses in the sidenotes on pages 16 and 104.

Danny

I had minimal doubts about being a counsellor. But those early clients didn't *do* quite as well as those now. I suspect that in the months and years ahead I will say that about today's clients. But I do feel good about me and I give them, me. Also I am aware I was fortunate; placements are not as forthcoming now for other students.

The experience of finding and securing a placement was dreadful. And student counselling placements were very poorly arranged. I was lucky enough to have access to clients privately which is something I had developed myself. Other students either had none or a few hours only. There was an attempt by our tutor to set up a student counselling service but this was poorly administrated and poorly marketed which meant it was rather disheartening for those who were trying to fulfil 'experiential hours' for the course criteria. My personal experience of

Philippa

counselling students is that they are much more challenging than non-students.

The experience of my first client was reasonable and certainly a great learning curve. I realised I needed more help in developing a professional approach to contracting. I operated from home which I did not like at all. It felt very unprofessional and I found I like to keep my workplace separate from my home environment, certainly with regard to personal safety. I did find a room to hire in a private practice but this had to be paid for which was difficult during training.

I didn't experience any significant problems with my placement clients, perhaps except clients not turning up after having made an appointment.

Robbie   There was a real scramble to get placements and thankfully our course had a tutor who was tasked with helping us find placements. I was lucky in that I managed to secure two separate placements; one was at a private therapy clinic where I saw 'low cost' clients and the second was at a GP practice. This provided me with an amazing contrast of clients. At the private clinic I predominantly saw more middle-class clients whose issues were more attuned to personal development via their presenting issue. At the GP practice I saw a less affluent clientele whose issues were life-crisis ones and more short-term.

Over the year, I became aware of the significant difference between venues of 'DNAs' (Did Not Attend). At the private clinic I would say the average was 20%, but at the GP practice more like 50–60%. I did notice that doctors had an equally frustrating time with people who did not turn up for appointments.

I was very fortunate with my counselling placements, being able to get two quite *Jan* near where I lived. One was a private centre, the other was one which was for women only. There was a tutor on our course who has responsibility for helping trainees find placements — he gave out addresses and contact names and the rest was up to us. I had interviews at both places and was given a briefing on how they operated.

I had a four-hour slot at both practices. At first the clients were slow in coming, especially at the women's practice, and I began to worry about the magic 100 hours [the course criteria for client contact hours] but slowly things improved. The frustration of clients not turning up was one thing I imagine most counsellors have experienced and it gives an unpredictability to the whole business. It reminded me of arranging private teacher tutoring in the past. (I remember I swore not to teach private classes because of the unreliability and it is ironic that I am now back in a similar position!)

Does everyone remember their first client? I don't think I will forget mine in a hurry. I was paralysed with fear and did not dare move a muscle for fear of doing something 'wrong'. Every time there was a silence I panicked about whether to speak or let it continue. Every time I spoke I thought 'what a stupid thing to say'. I was very aware of needing to behave *like a counsellor*.

Steff   The struggle to get a placement was symptomatic of trying to get a counselling job at the end of the course. Both were elusive and I had to throw myself at counselling contexts which were not where I wanted to work but in the former case I wanted the experience and in the latter I needed the money.

The process of setting up a counselling experience for me began a couple of months *Charlie* before my course was due to begin. I was exploring several placement opportunities that would fulfil my interests and needs as well as the requirements of the course, when a women's health organisation was suggested to me by the course coordinator, along with other helpful suggestions. The reasons for arranging this placement against others were based on my initial meeting (with their counsellor and line manager), my sound interest in the organisation's clients and services (health care for women) and the organisation's well-developed and established counselling service which worked within the BAC Code of Ethics. There was also no pressure on me to limit the number of sessions available to clients or to increase my caseload due to a pressing waiting-list.

Early in September of that year, there was a team meeting for all the new and previous counsellors which created a feeling of belonging and support for me. I also gained a better understanding of the organisation's written policy, standardised procedures and set of guidelines for counsellors. (That was also the day I received my first referral!) Furthermore, I believe that the interaction between my training course and the organisation gave me a sense of security and added further support. Meeting with my supervisor (from the course) and my line manager did enhance the integrity of my placement from the beginning. Last but not least, I found the counsellor (who was person-centred) of the organisation very supportive and available. At the times I needed help I felt heard and was treated as a colleague and a valued member of the team.

In retrospect, the main frustration I experienced was that there wasn't much flexibility in hours and availability in rooms due to the pressure of all the other services, as the counselling service was recognised but still a rather small part of what the organisation offered and somewhat affected by the interventions of 'higher authorities'. However, later on I grew to understand that the stress related to the room-bookings had made quite a positive contribution to my increased capacity to handle ambiguity.

Also, my first direct experience of the counselling rooms was rather disappointing, as they looked quite clinical and austere with a strong smell of antiseptic. I was aware of the overall dynamics of the organisation, the medical setting I was in and also of the general atmosphere which was quite informal, open and friendly. What helped me to cope more creatively with my first impressions of the rooms was the time I decided to spend in them, arranging and rearranging the medical items and furniture. This also eased some of the tension of the early days of my placement.

Ronnie   I remember thoughout my training placement that I had an unhelpful thorn in the overall experience. This was the course criteria to meet a specified number of client counselling hours in order to get the Diploma. I know this is necessary and

I can't see any way round this. But periods when few referrals came through were tense as I kept my eye on a fairly static client tally count. I was also frustrated by clients who didn't turn up and possibly more so because of the pressure to gain these hours. This was something I wrestled with in supervision as I tried to make sure this frustration did not spill over into the client relationships. This supervision also made me reflect on whether I was doing anything to influence the 'no-shows'. Generally, I wasn't, but I learnt to communicate a more solid and professional contracting arrangement with clients which did reduce the 'no-shows'.

But I reflected back on this some time after completing (and passing) my Diploma when I was working as a counsellor. Interestingly, I found as a salaried part-time student counsellor there was a complete absence of the pressure I had during the placement. Ironically, my 'no-shows' were a mere 1%, very very few clients did not turn up. I know this could be the result of many things, good referrals, my improved skills, my being more relaxed, me being salaried whether people turned up or not etc.

However, I have also been working privately and because they pay me, I find I have new pressures. I contract that if they want to cancel, they need to give me at least 24 hours notice otherwise I charged them 50% of the session fee. Ironically, I get very few who miss an appointment or who don't phone me, rather some who cancel about 25 hours before their next appointment! My supervisor is kept well informed of this.

Geoffrey

I had quite a scary time during my placement period because I had a client who said that she felt like she was falling in love with me. In any other situation I would have been flattered and grateful for such a confidence boost but in the counselling context this really caused me great distress. I became very defensive and withdrawn in the sessions and even with more frequent supervision to support me during this period, I still don't feel I handled this very well. In the end, we decided to terminate counselling. In retrospect, I think I was unwilling to 'work through' the issue. This I regret.

points to ponder

• Determine the course requirements before arranging a placement. It is important to confirm that the counselling placement of your choice fulfils the criteria of your course. There is a variety of different types of placements around: student counselling offered by many universities and colleges, GP practice, individual private practice, private therapy centres, placements which focus on one issue, such as, bereavement, substance use, HIV and AIDS, gender, sexuality, relationships, physical health and mental health.

• Each placement will offer a different experience and challenge. In the case-studies, Robbie highlighted his differing experience of two placements: 'At the private clinic I predominantly saw more middle-class clients whose issues were more attuned to personal development via their presenting issue. At the GP practice I saw a less "affluent" clientele whose issues were life crisis ones and more short-term.'

• Check out the number of client contact hours required to fulfil the criteria of your course. It is important to be clear on this point. It is an area which can cause trainees some concern. As Jan states, 'At first the clients were slow in coming, especially at the women's practice, and I began to worry about the magic 100 hours [her course criterion for client contact hours] but slowly things improved.'

• Discuss with your individual supervisor how to manage your work and how to get support from them, your line manager or placement manager. Look at Chapter 11 'Supervision' for more details.

Tony Merry looks at supervision for person-centred counsellors and trainees in his book *Learning and Being in Person-Centred Counselling,* pages 137–156. The full reference for this, and other useful books, is given in Appendix 2.

• Ask trainers, staff or placement personnel how they were with their first clients. This will help you realise that it is a tense experience for most people. The first session can be a difficult and challenging experience for the client too! It may be their first contact with a counsellor. It can also be a special and joyous process of starting your journey as a counsellor and working with your client to explore their pathway.

• Explain to your client in the first session your status (i.e. that of trainee) duration of time you are committed to the placement, length of session, supervision and confidentiality.

• Clarify the placement and your expectations if the client requires to cancel an appointment. The case-studies highlight interesting issues for counsellors when a client cancels or does not attend the session.

• Check out from your placement venue any particular policies, procedures, rules and regulations or legal obligations related to the client group which you must comply with, for instance with referrals or with regard to confidentiality. Your main responsibility is to your client but you may have responsibilities to your organisation and to the law. You will need to work out how you can appropriately satisfy all these criteria.

You will find that each placement agency has its own 'rules'. If your placement is in a statutory agency (e.g. the Health Service, Social Services, or a school), you will find that certain legal obligations pertain, such as the Children Act in schools.

11 supervision

Supervision is defined by the British Association for Counselling in the Code of Ethics & Practice, January 1998 (under review), in three clauses;

B.6.3.1. Counselling supervision refers to a formal agreement which enables counsellors to discuss their counselling regularly with one or more people who are normally experienced as counselling practitioners and have an understanding of counselling supervision. Its purpose is to ensure the efficacy of the counsellor-client relationship. It is a confidential relationship.

B.6.3.2.The counselling supervisor role should, wherever possible, be independent of the line manager role. However, where the counselling supervisor is also the line manager, the counsellor must have regular access to independent counselling supervision.

Counselling supervision offers the counsellor the opportunity to maintain and develop their practice through discussion of issues related to their clients. The supervisor should be someone who is independent of the counsellor. A line manager is not an appropriate counselling supervisor. A line manager has responsibility to the overall service in addition to the individual counsellor and clients of the service. It would be unlikely that he/she would be able to offer the impartial and confidential relationship which the counsellor requires.

A supervisor is able to offer you their experience and knowledge of counselling practice in order to assist in any issues which arise in your work. A supervisor can assist you in gaining insight into issues relating to your client and the person-centred counsellor's approach is heavily influenced by the use of self, since the supervisor will also be facilitating personal development issues with you.

Supervision can be a safe place to begin to challenge yourself and your work as a counsellor. This may challenge your approach, use of the core conditions and any blind spots which become apparent. It is important to choose a supervisor that you can trust and with whom you feel able to be honest and open. Only you can identify the qualities which will allow you to feel both supported and stimulated in this relationship.

There are different forms of supervision — individual, group, peer and internal (or self-supervision). The BAC (see sidenotes) recommends that the amount of supervision undertaken should 'reflect the volume of counselling work undertaken and the experience of the counsellor'. COSCA (formerly the Confederation of Scottish Counselling Agencies) make a similar recommendation. A good supervisor will be able to help a counsellor work out an appropriate amount of supervision in accordance with the current guidelines.

Individual Supervision is time spent one-to-one with a supervisor who will be an experienced practising counsellor.

Group supervision requires an identified supervisor-facilitator and some others, possibly other counsellors (maybe in your placement) or peers (maybe from your course). In training, you will probably be involved in group supervision which may be facilitated by course staff. This can be a valuable source of supervision in that it offers you a pool of different experience and values, is helpful in hearing other counsellors' approaches to a particular problem and this can widen your way of viewing situations.

Peer supervision can take place one-to-one or in a group. It involves discussing your work with counsellors of similar experience to yourself where either of you can take on the roles of supervisor and supervisee as required. This sometimes happens in workplace settings where colleagues, taking turns to be the 'supervisor', can offer feedback on client work .

Internal supervision (or self-supervision) is a process which is integral to all of the above forms of supervision. The counsellor monitors their current psychological state, own way of working and personal response to clients, as well as highlighting when additional one-to-one supervision sessions might be prudent. Sometimes, it may be your supervisor who recognises your reaction or response to a particular client or your attitude to your practice, and your supervisor will work with you in exploring this further. It may be that you will want to look at the issue at depth. Personal therapy can be a useful place where you can focus on personal development with regards to difficult issues brought up by clients.

At one stage, Laura's supervisor noticed that the content of her supervision focused completely on her clients — she saw few, if any, personal issues coming up in the supervision session. When her supervisor mentioned this, Laura thought very little of it but after the supervision session had finished she became aware of the relevance of this observation. Laura was ignoring a personal issue and pushing it to one side hoping it would stay there until she had time to 'deal with it'. Laura began to work on this issue in personal counselling and by addressing this she was able to be more open and responsive in the counselling process.

Rick remembers one significant issue which he explored in depth with his personal supervisor. This related to his wrestling with the difference between 'interpretation' and 'intuition'. He was unsure whether in some cases he was making interpretations with a client and this seemed to jar with what he felt to be appropriate. It transpired that this concern was more about his process of continually policing and evaluating his practice.

All types of supervision, whether individual or group, are the key to continual professional development for you as a counsellor. When you finish training you will find supervision becomes the major learning mechanism.

B.6.3.3. Counselling supervision must be regular, consistent and appropriate to the counselling. The volume should reflect the volume of counselling work undertaken and the experience of the counsellor.

Shona I found peer supervision very useful, certainly in groups of about four or six. One-to-one supervision was essential but I think it is best to have both. For me, peer supervision was more challenging than the one-to-one work, so I was more likely to become aware of potential difficulties arising from blindspots to some dynamic of the client/counsellor relationship.

I only had one real problem with my individual supervisor when her boundaries were poor for one session. This made me realise that I had been relying on her to maintain boundaries for me, so the experience led me to maintain my own more.

Overall this was a very useful experience.

Finding an individual supervisor was easy though difficult to fund. I found being a supervisee an enlightening experience where much learning took place. I didn't always like the sessions if there was something going on for me but they were always full of information, helpful and essential when dealing with real and practice clients. I gained more awareness of what I was doing, how I was perceiving them, transferred feelings from old relationships and automatic ways of behaving. It made me question my impact, interpretation and interference.

Jenny

Group supervision is an excellent way of testing things out — though at ten my group was quite large and great self-discipline was needed. I felt I could hog the group every week quite easily.

Finding an individual supervisor was quite easy as we were given a list of suitable ones. It is hard to know from one interview who is best for you. I am not sure how well I connect with my supervisor, or how she sees me. At the very beginning of seeing clients I got into a panic as I gave my client my phone number and then regretted it. I phoned my supervisor for support (as she had said contact outside sessions was OK) but came off the phone feeling more dreadful than before. I raised it at the next meeting and feel it was just not knowing each other and how we operate.

Apart from that, my experience of supervision has been very positive although I find the hour every two weeks flies past and I would like to spend an hour discussing each client!

Gaby

I know we need individual supervisors but I dislike what seems to be the usual cosy, incestuous counselling world. Many of the trainers are also supervisors and they are the ones with jobs, whilst the rest of us end up keeping them in business and us out?!

Linn

For my own counselling work, I have experienced both group and one-to-one supervision and I must say that I did not find the group I was part of terribly helpful. It was not that the people in the groups were unhelpful or unsupportive but it was more to do with feeling that there was never enough time. I was often left wondering whether I was denying something in my feeling of there being 'no problems at the moment' but there was never enough time to explore whether or not this was an accurate assessment or not! At the moment I am working on a one-to-one basis with someone who has been my supervisor for the last three years. She is very supportive, encouraging as well as being challenging, all offered from a person-centred base and I feel very safe and affirmed by her.

Grahame

My group supervision became quite strained. Eventually someone challenged the whole group for being very twee, nice and unchallenging. This may have involved the tutor facilitator but it was ongoing. There were some strong personalities and I got annoyed when I was volunteering my observations and the person seemed totally unable to take on board my comments, unwilling to question their actions or motives. Were we all trying to 'appear' the expert? Often personal issues came out for people and I found this frustrating as there was so little time for group supervision and I wanted this to be the focus. There was after all a place — a group where personal issues could be aired.

My individual supervisor proved much more useful and I have been with my supervisor ever since. I question myself harshly and critically in a way that actually feels right, I have become my own best supervisor but this has been facilitated by the skills, insight, experience and the trust which has built up with my individual supervisor.

Kathleen

When I was about to see my first client and my course was due to begin, I opted to use my first supervision hour (out of the eight that my course offered which I found useful to increase to thirteen) as an opportunity to explore my anxieties, hopes and fears and to discuss possible ways of presenting myself, describing my task and the terms of counselling to my client. That was the beginning of a very good relationship I gradually developed with my supervisor.

I believe that a critical part of my development was my experience of submitting my interactions with clients to scrutiny during personal and group supervision. Addressing and confronting my feelings, thoughts, attitudes and frustrations (which turned out to be invaluable for me) enabled me to grow in self-understanding, awareness, self-acceptance and confidence and to work more effectively with my clients. I needed to be free to make mistakes, to explore and experiment and at the same time take responsibility for myself. It was in supervision that I learned that I can make mistakes without losing my self-respect.

Easing up my pace and recognising my need for personal limits was a learning that came from my interaction with and feedback from several people, including my personal tutor and my supervisor. Making space for me in that stressful process was the starting point in questioning my boundaries, monitoring the process of my development and in enjoying the way towards my goal.

Andy

My supervisor was a right plonker. I just did not like him. We met up for a trial 'session' and he seemed OK but as I got into a supervision relationship he just kept on telling me what I should be doing or what I shouldn't be doing. He never explored issues or questioned me, he used statements from his obviously massive intellect and vast experience to TELL me what to do. I changed my supervisor after three months. My two regrets as I write this is that I took three months to change and also that I can't mention his name because I really want to put other people off him. He was very disruptive to my learning.

Sally

I don't know what I would do without my individual supervisor. I've worked with him for six years. He has been my sounding board, my guide, my inspiration and mentor. I have often come with quite difficult issues and stressful concerns yet he's been supportive, helpful and astute in his supervising.

points to ponder

Tony Merry looks at supervision for person-centred counsellors and trainees in his book *Learning and Being in Person-Centred Counselling,* pages 137–156. The full reference for this, and other useful books, is given in Appendix 2.

• Determine what criteria the course has with regard to finding and choosing an individual supervisor.

• You may like to meet with a number of potential individual supervisors before making your choice. This will give you a choice as to who might be most appropriate for you. Ask them about their supervision experience, confidentiality, background, motivations, fee structure and options for making contact in addition to the formalised contract. The 'contract' is usually a verbal agreement of responsibilities you will both have, such as keeping appointments, cancellations, frequency of visits etc.

• Your supervisor will almost certainly become a major source of learning and development, therefore, it is crucial that you can relate to each other in the way that is most useful to you.

• When choosing an appropriate supervisor it can be useful to ask about their counselling work. For instance, ask whether they have certain client groups with which they have difficulty working in case this impacts on your own client work.

• Confirm the boundaries in place for group supervision work. Is everyone clear about confidentiality? If you are unhappy with this, what can you do or say to make it better for you?

• Is there a way in which everyone can contribute equally to the time allocated for group supervision?

• Clarify with your peers and facilitator a boundary between *client* work and *personal* work and discuss a happy medium, one which respects issues which will come up for people whilst not detracting from the short time allocated to the supervision focus.

• Supervision can become a key mechanism for learning. Shona found it a 'very useful experience', Jenny felt group supervision was 'an excellent way of testing things out' and Linn seemed very happy with her supervisor who was 'very supportive, encouraging as well as being challenging, all from a person-centred base'. Linn felt 'safe and affirmed by her'.

• Consider what you want from supervision. Is it to sort out counselling dilemmas, to get confirmation that what you are doing is right or to advance your knowledge of theory and skills practice? Perhaps it's all of these. Ask not what you can do for supervision but what can supervision do for you!

• Consider your client/counsellor nightmare scenario and think about how you might prepare for this!

The introduction to Section B suggested that one of the most difficult tasks we face in the process of communication is that of relating to and interacting with other people. This section is dedicated to looking at the influence that counselling training can have on relationships with our partners, family and friends.

Many trainees notice that a strong bond is created during training between course participants, including tutors. Counselling training courses are very unusual environments, sometimes experienced as separate from and artificial in comparison to the reality of everyday life. For others, it may seem very real. It can be a supportive, caring, challenging and helping group where people are able to share some of their deepest concerns, worries, dreams and secrets. It is unlikely you will experience such an environment like this again, except for future training courses or counselling group work. This closeness and intimacy can be both a seductive and precious feeling as much for its humaneness as for its uncommonness. For some this can represent a new way of being, a new way of relating and communicating to one another, whilst for others this represents an ideal which is far removed from the realities of modern living and they are content to see it as utopia.

We will be relating to, and interacting with, our course peers in a way which might not be either possible or *safe* in the outside world. Again, this is part of the learning process, to be able to mix and manage the two worlds in which we live during the training — the course world and the outside world. We may find the course an 'oasis', a 'heaven' even and it can be frustrating that the rest of the world is not like this. This can be an insight which can cause us to re-manage our relationships and lives in a way that does try to emulate the course experience. Some succeed in doing this, others have great difficulty.

Chapter 12 starts with a review of the impact that our fellow trainees might have on us, our peers and classmates. They will become both our mirrors and our models, reflecting what we like and dislike as they, too, battle through the demands of the training experience, confronting their fears and anxieties. We will support them as they will support us. There may be times when we do not want to support them and they do not want to offer us support. The widest range of relating and communication can become a reality as trainees explore their way along the path of the course.

Chapter 13 looks at the influence that counselling training can have on the relationship for trainees who have partners. It might be a useful point to make here, that counselling training is frequently described in highs and lows. The reality may be a rollercoaster for some, but importantly there will also be bland, possibly boring bits — times when you just can't be bothered to get into the work when you just want to sit and observe, or sit and disconnect, or just go home! The focus of this particular chapter is to describe not only some of the problems experienced, but also some of the positive and rewarding impacts on trainees' partners.

The family is the topic for Chapter 14. We all have a set of family relationships which have built up since our birth and which, invariably, will influence how we think, feel and behave with each other. Counselling training will affect these dynamics as many of the case-studies will reveal. The training may also enable people to share the happy and sad sides of their past and present lives. This sharing can help open up a new understanding about our own families and how living as a family has etched itself onto our psyches.

The final chapter in this section, Chapter 15 provides an illuminating series of accounts that give us an insight into the changes which have occurred for some former trainees with regard to their friends or friendships. We may experience a new dimension to relationships we form with people on our course. Our actual friends outside the course may not change, but we may alter the way we relate to and communicate with them. Maybe we will be seeking a greater kind of depth of relating, maybe not. Counselling does not, and perhaps should not, make us 'heavy, deep and overly introspective' people, rather we can choose how we want to be from the well-stocked arsenal of our self-awareness. In this way, we can choose how we connect with people.

12 the influence of course peers

Laura felt that her relationships with colleagues was a fundamental part of training and her life experience. It was an experience that she'll never forget. All of the relationships stay with her and even today she is learning from them. Some of the relationships went on to develop and deepen. Others physically finished with the end of the course but are still with her in other ways — she finds that a memory of a discussion or a scenario will pop into her mind at different times. Laura now realises that she hadn't grasped fully what was going on at the time but a couple of years later it became more clear (an amazing feeling!). She feels that the relationships made with fellow trainees will be lifelong.

Why were Laura's fellow trainees so influential in her training? Why do they continue to offer her inspiration? For her, the relationships she formed then had an intensity and vibrancy which were very stimulating. They offered her a blend of stimulation coupled with a solid quality of support — a fantastic combination which helped her to explore many issues that previously she had felt too frightened to explore. The combination of stimulating challenge and support was essential. Support on its own may have lulled her into a cosy corner. Constant challenge may have left her feeling exhausted and in fighting mode — she felt that she had experienced the core conditions from many of her colleagues. For many, including herself, it was difficult to be empathic, accepting and real but she appreciated it even more by recognising the struggle that people often experienced in trying to offer the core conditions.

In counselling training we get the chance to really relate to one another in a way which can seem quite different from what we are used to. The majority of training courses have between 15 and 30 participants. This number can usually offer a wide mix of backgrounds and life experiences. During the course of the training, we are likely to share many intimate details about ourselves and this will also be reciprocated. The level of intimacy for this number of people can create a very close bonding. Furthermore, we are all striving to learn about counselling, we have a common goal and purpose. But within this we will be travelling separate and individual journeys to self-discovery, learning about who we are. Our peers will contribute heavily to this quest.

Rick was quite taken aback by the level of intimacy generated by his course. He was a single man on a course with a predominance of women. This, in itself, was very challenging for him, though he would have liked a more even ratio. (He still wonders why there seem to be many more women who go into counselling than men.) However, what happened to Rick was probably not a consequence of this gender imbalance. He developed a love for a fellow trainee on his course. It started as a result of the deep level of sharing, support, companionship and camaraderie that he had only ever before experienced, to the same degree, with a partner. He wrestled with whether he should tell the woman concerned his feelings or not. She had recently started a relationship with a new partner and so Rick didn't want to stir this up. But his feelings towards her were very important. Withholding this would have meant hiding a significant part of himself. He also thought, despite the risks involved, that she might understand his feelings and that this would be good for them both to discuss openly — so he went ahead and told her how he felt. The result of the subsequent chat was that they each could understand where the other was coming from. Since then they have been very close friends. He still loves her and knows this is reciprocal, without any complicating feelings of jealousy, rejection and possession. Where they're both lucky is that they can have this close connection in addition to their current life-partners.

Sharing this experience with you is not intended to suggest that such activities are part of the course but to illustrate the depth of connection we can achieve with our peers. In fact, on the other side of the scale, Rick found a couple of individuals whom he could not understand or relate to — in fact he actually disliked them. He was eventually able to talk openly with one of them, sensing a reciprocity, and they both used this to great effect, learning much from this exchange. They didn't improve their friendship but they understood each other differently and were content to hold and respect each other's views. Rick regrets not having spoken to the other individual, and the lost opportunity for contact and learning.

Our peers will become an influential part of training, at every level. Their insight, sharing and learning will facilitate a new level of understanding and development. As some of the following case-studies illustrate, such experiences can be positive and negative but all will contribute to increased leaning about ourselves, about others and about relating.

Julie

There was a difficult relationship with another student in the third year, someone that several of us had difficulties with, which left me reeling and in great emotional distress. It made me question all my concepts and working practice and whilst this was in itself positive, the experience was very disturbing, for I have had to come to terms with the fact that this relationship remains unresolved. I did not experience a coming together or a feeling of wholeness, which of course is something I want in life, love and the world at large.

There were about five people with whom I became extremely close on the course. They supported yet challenged me. Without this help and support I feel it would have been impossible to 'stay with' and work through all the issues which came up for me. Apart from the above student, those peers with whom I found myself in conflict with became closer as we worked through issues together, teaching us much about ourselves and others.

Clifford   I was aware during my course that we were not feeling as a group; we were professional but still trainees. However, there was a feeling that this was not quite right and that an embryonic professionalism was emerging.

In my first year, I established close working relationships with others easily. There was a sense of sharing the experience of being a student and sharing experiences and revelations about oneself. There was some friction, though generally with others who pushed sensitive buttons in me. This awareness enabled me to understand how this affected my ability to see them as themselves. In my second year I moved to another group. This was more difficult and has taken longer to establish closer relationships.

There was a great deal of support from other trainees throughout the course —   *Jane*
this was extremely valuable to me. Although there were inevitably some conflicts
amongst individuals at times, the overall feeling was of a group working together,
helping each other and giving time to each other when needed.

Mike   We were all in a state of development at different stages of *willingness to experience*. So it was like a pendulum at times. Sometimes I would get on brilliantly with people, supporting them and being there for them, and at other times I would be the one wanting this support. The other constant challenge for me was in noticing some students who seemed clearly unable or unwilling to become proficient counsellors, usually through some monumental defence mechanism. This meant me fighting with my knowledge of being judgemental against that of feeling responsible to me and them, to challenge this. I am not 'the' expert, but I would have hoped my comments might have been valuable. In retrospect, I still feel several peers got off lightly and I regret not having been more forceful and assertive with my observations. They are practising counsellors today and that worries me.

In my experience most people I have come across on various counselling courses,   *Jennifer*
but particularly on the Diploma, have been groups of very supportive people. I
also feel that person-centred counselling courses, in their offering of the 'Core
Conditions' and emphasis on relationships and self-awareness, lend themselves
to the development of intimacy and allowing people to be who they are. In fact, I
am still in contact with four people who I developed particularly close relationships
with as a result of being part of the same Professional Development Group. They
are now very valued friends and colleagues.

Daniel   My father died just at the end of my first year of study. I was glad I had the wide person-centred family around me, for I was heard and I wanted to share with them.

I like solitude but I miss people and so try to balance my wants and likes. I have internally questioned some peers to facilitate an understanding and used them as I have been used — for that *safe place* was the place to practise.

I had, I believe, good fortune in my *personal partnerships*. We all worked and made a commitment. That was valuable, showing each other to be worthy, open and supportive. Taking some of the loneliness out of things, aiding understanding as the depth of reading deepened, enabling views to be seen from other perceptions.

John

Conditions to learn. We sat in a circle. We always started sat in a circle. Counsellorly. And we began the process of listening to each other, and listening to ourselves. Do we really listen to each other or are we always listening to ourselves through the lives and words of others?

I sat in a personal development group. I said that my greatest fear was to have a client who disclosed that they had sexually abused a child, and know, that as a survivor, I was going to have to face working with an abuser. The group sat there, and then talked about the weather. There was no challenge to the manoeuvre within the group.

There was no empathy. There was judgement. And I found I could not be true. I lost my hard-fought-for sense of self.

Sam

Out of the 29 people on the course there was only one with whom I had difficulty relating to, on his own and in groups. I found him false and could feel myself being false in reply. I spent a lot of energy trying to get over this — telling myself that I don't need to like him, just respect him and accept how he is. I know I have improved but I know that if I meet him in another context outwith the course I would classify him as obnoxious!

The Community Groups were a challenging place to speak and I did not do this very often though I tried to find them as safe as the smaller groups. Some course members expressed strong emotions in the large group — love, anger — and I felt OK with that and envied their ability to be themselves in the group.

Angie

Whilst I was training to become a counsellor my feelings ranged between deeply painful and ecstatically joyful. Being with a group of fourteen to eighteen people for three days, eight times a year gave me a sense of family that supported me during the *ordinary* times when I was at work.

My peer group, with whom I trained, came from a variety of backgrounds; differences in race, colour, sex, sexuality, age, professions and abilities. In my first year I had difficulties being patient with some people. I struggled to be unconditionally positively regarding towards and empathic with them. Some people reminded me of abusive relationships from my past. My way of coping with that was to steel myself to work with them. I hoped to dispel my illusion that they would *behave* in the same way and thereby elicit the same responses from me. The more this worked for me, the less I avoided conflict and confrontation in ways I had developed to protect myself in the past. Morning and evening 'check-ins/outs' every day of the course helped this process. This became almost the most important part of the *training* for me. It was how I learned to trust myself and my peers and that the trainer would be facilitative and not intrusive nor rescuing.

Sheila   The end of one particular experience, coupled with a wonderfully supportive, accepting Personal Development Group gave me a much stronger sense of self and a much higher level of both self-awareness and self-acceptance. It also helped me to discover that my most often used defence mechanism of anger was, in fact, a denial of the pain and hurt that was often underneath the anger. It was easier to deny my pain and get angry than to feel the pain or let others see it.

The best part of the course for me was, without a shadow of a doubt, the Personal Development Group. There were eight members including the facilitator. Their love, acceptance, understanding and non-judgementalism brought much healing and wholeness to me. Yet they still challenged me but not critically. They might not always agree with me but I was entitled to my opinion as they were entitled to theirs. It felt great to be ME!

My early problems with a course member brought a sense of realism to the learning   *George*
and as I struggled with feelings. I evaluated behaviours in such a way as to take
responsibility for those feelings, as solely mine. I can smile now as I wonder if the
other person had any idea what was going on. I don't think he did as he went on to
upset others after me.

• It is likely that you will experience a variety of emotions towards your course colleagues. Throughout your training you are not only learning much about yourself but also about your fellow trainees. The focus on interaction with your course colleagues is a fundamental way of learning in person-centred training.

points to ponder

• Your peers are going through change too. For some it will be more traumatic and dramatic than for others.

• Be available to offer support to someone when in need. You never know when you will want the same in return.

• If someone annoys or upsets you, only you can decide the next step. But you can seek help in making the decision. Family, friends, peer groups, tutors, personal development groups, supervision, and community groups are all potential places to discuss the problem. You may feel it is an issue strictly for you and the person you have a difficulty with and choose to address it privately. Or you may wish to raise it in a group on your course. It can be difficult and painful to confront a problem in this way but the rewards and learning can be profound, for you and often for others involved in the process.

• Because of the intimacy, intensity and level of sharing between you and your colleagues, do not be surprised if you develop feelings of real love towards them. This can be frightening to become aware of, but also reminds us of the possibility that this could happen wherever there are intense feelings, even in a client/counsellor relationship.

• You may well develop a real dislike for someone. This happens.

• John shares his experience which seemed quite upsetting, 'There was no empathy. There was judgement.' Sam reached a realisation that she disliked a peer, 'I found him false and could feel myself being false in reply . . . I know if I meet him in another context outwith the course I would classify him as obnoxious!'

• Several former trainees look back on how they were with peers and a common regret is that 'something was never said'. A training course only lasts for a specific period of time — make the most of the valuable resource of your peers to learn about yourself and them.

13
the impact
upon my
partner

This chapter seeks to highlight how partners of trainees cope with the effects of the counselling training. As with the other chapters in this section on *interpersonal relationships*, it is not just the trainee who is faced with changes or who tries to wade through a sea of new relationships and intense self-awareness. A trainee is likely to seek support from, and confide in, their partner about many aspects of the counselling training — triumphs in skills practise, emotionally draining workshops, or dramatic personal insights. As we learn more about ourselves we may begin to choose to make changes to how we are or how we behave with people. In this sense, we may choose to *change* elements of who we are and this will undoubtedly affect how we are with our partners.

Some of the case-studies in this chapter reveal how counselling training really strengthens a relationship, while others highlight the training as the spark which ends it. It is unlikely that a relationship deteriorates *as a result* of training on its own, rather any positive or negative angle is likely to be magnified or exaggerated. A significant amount of self-exploration and self-awareness takes place during training, which means we have the opportunity to reflect on how we feel about ourselves, consider our values and beliefs and determine what changes we might like to make in order to become 'better' people.

The degree of exploration the trainee undertakes during training can feel threatening to a partner. In fact, it may not be the level of exploration but the potential degree of change which may arise from an increase in self-awareness. The partner can experience feelings of losing control and stability of their relationship. An important factor helping your partner is *effective communication.*

During the course it might be that we choose to invest greater time, effort and commitment into our relationship. Since training may encourage us to change, it can be difficult enough just coping with this, let alone trying to share it with a partner — our partner may be happy enough with the person we once were. Some partners believe the changes in the person with whom they are involved have turned them into quite a different person from the one they first met. In many cases it seems that it is up to the trainee to be aware of the effect their counselling training might have on their partner and to communicate this appropriately.

A useful area that Laura's partner picked up on was related to 'jargon'. During training, Laura acquired a new vocabulary which was completely acceptable in a counselling culture, but to the ears of others it would sound alien, unintelligible and elitist. This observation enabled Laura to become aware of her language and how it sounded outside the counselling arena. It helped her to focus on keeping her language simple and appropriate to the 'real world'.

It may be helpful in your relationship to discuss the issue of communication, prior to starting training. Although there is no best way and each relationship has different needs, it is important to keep each other informed as to change in awareness, beliefs, attitudes and aspirations for the future. Your partner may also be able to offer insights into any changes in you which they notice.

The *depth* of new relationships formed with peers on the course can cause stress to existing relationships as partners wrestle with a challenge to their previously unrivalled intimacy. Perhaps it is more a question of a *different* type of relationship rather than a *deeper* one. Making a differentiation can sometimes help us find our way around the new meanings of relationships made during training.

Intimacy between you and a partner may be a private experience in that this is the main person with whom you share important and significant issues. Your partner may find it disturbing to discover the heightened level of intimacy you experience with fellow course members. Sometimes the fear is that intimacy with your partner will be reduced, threatened or eroded. Sometimes it is the fear that it may be less 'sacred' or exclusive. You may feel the need to prepare your partner for this and this may be an issue which you can continue to discuss throughout your training.

Several people who have gone through training also claim that as they learned more about themselves, discovering different or more defined values and beliefs, they became unwilling to settle for their original or current relationship. Some people may have paddled along with an 'OK' relationship but the training instilled in them a greater sense of self-respect, self-confidence and independence which could lead to them wanting more, and eventually ending their long-standing relationship.

Our partners should not be expected to understand the training, they only hear from us second-hand and they are not physically on the course. Perhaps the challenge for trainees is to test out newly developed counselling skills so that we can clearly hear and understand the fears, worries and misunderstandings about which our partners tell us. Hopefully, we can articulate our training experience in a more sensitive way.

However, it is important to be aware of the difference between listening and trying to understand our partners and offering our partners counselling. In training, we are attempting to integrate the counselling approach into our way of being, and, we must be careful not to stray into trying to offer our partners counselling rather than simply being a sensitive and understanding companion.

The majority of contributors were in relationships during their training and this is borne out by the emphasis in the case-studies. However, some respondents were single and it should go without saying that this can raise completely different relationship issues.

Dwight My soul mate was brave and stuck by me, not understanding what was going on, wishing I would not punish myself but not knowing all the time that it was *the challenge I needed*. I allowed me to be me and this openness allowed others to be closer. My world became warmer and bigger. My soul mate risked it, worked at understanding the pain.

My partner found my being on the course very hard going much of the time. Not only because of the time I spent on written work but because of the emotional distress I often found myself in. There were long phone calls to supportive peers and long discussions with him about my feelings. He very seldom backed away from supporting me but I know it was a strain on him.   *Elspeth*

Initially when I began training he felt I was examining everything he said for its hidden meaning. This is still something I deny. Although this has now stopped, I used to be told one of two things when in conflict with him, depending on what he was trying to resolve or get; 'You should understand me because you're a counsellor', or, 'I am not a client, don't counsel me'.

Diana There has always been meaningful commitment in the relationship with my partner which enabled each of us to stand by the other in periods of stress and distress. During my training course, particularly during the Diploma year, I was often absent for him and he was very understanding and respectful of the space I needed to make for me at the time. I highly valued his unfailing support and help during the difficult times which, amongst other things, enabled me to reach my goal.

Briefly, we both agree that my training experience has had a profound impact on our relationship in that we are increasingly spending more time together, talking more freely about ourselves. We are sharing and exploring our feelings, perceptions, wishes, worst fears and fantasies. The quality of our being together is changing. We are both growing and I feel I am learning from him as much as he is learning from me.

His personal comments about the time I was in training include that the constant emphasis on self-knowledge and my expectation for mutual exploration put certain amounts of pressure on him. He also found my 'way of being' too serious and missed having fun together. For him, it was a challenging and rewarding experience to see me growing, and still is.

I was also surprised at the impact outside the course that the changes in me brought about. I was no longer able to put up with some of my partner's behaviour. As a result I split up with him and I have no regrets. I decided that I deserve to be treated better than he was able or willing to treat me.   *Jules*

Rebecca My partner has been very supportive while I have been on the course. He has done his best to understand when I come home in a soggy heap. However, as with any topic, I have to watch myself that he does not get every minute of the day recounted to him in minute detail. When I felt I needed to start personal counselling we discussed this and the issues that I felt I needed to look at more closely than was possible on the course. Initially he felt that a few sessions was OK but that more would indicate there was something wrong which I was not discussing with him and he felt quite threatened by this, so a lot of work and discussion has gone into this. He has not noticed any major changes in me since I started the course, although he feels that I now look at my relationships within my family (with my mother and sister especially) in a clearer way.

Donald

There has been an impact on my partner. We have had to reassess our own relationship, how we cope with new close friendships that demand time, time away from our marriage. We have had to re assess how we communicate with each other and our friends.

The process of training brought me life. And has taken us (do counsellors ever really take seriously 'significant others'?) into an utterly new way of living. This is not stress free. We have had to go through regular depressions; we have, are, wrestling with newly born identities. We are not as sure as we used to be.

Roger I was single throughout the period of my full-time Diploma. This brought different pressures that many of my partnered peers did not have to deal with, and for sure, vice versa. I did not have to smooth a way through course and partner. But my focus on the type of relationship sought did change. I started to believe I could only ever go out with a counsellor, only she could connect with me in the same way I would want to with her. I have had brief encounters with people not connected with counselling and these just have not worked out. Is it that I now have too high a set of expectations and demands? If I do, then the training has much to blame. I wish I could 'settle' for someone less and then build, but this is a real struggle.

Andrea

I can't comment on my partner's comments about changes to me but the training has certainly helped us to establish and maintain a relationship despite external difficulties. We are able to use quite a lot of the counselling framework to share our feelings, thoughts and wishes with each other. Even very difficult ones. So from that point of view it has been an enormous help. But this doesn't always seem to work with my children though!!

Pauline I feel as if I'm in a new relationship even after 18 years of marriage. We don't talk to each other anymore . . . we talk *with* each other!

• Counselling training may put a strain on the relationship with your partner.

• It will probably help to be able to prepare your relationship for your training experience — so talk about it beforehand with your partner.

• You may like to discuss with your partner some issues which might come up, such as:
  • changes to your values and beliefs
  • the need for personal counselling
  • changes in your confidence, assertiveness and behaviour
  • the need for you to have time and space to yourself
  • that they probably will not be able to do anything to make the course less stressful
  • the emotional and physical energy needed for training and
  • the effect on your respective family and friends

• Your partner might not understand what counselling, or the training, is about and so may need to rely on you to offer an explanation.

• You might like to consider allocating time to spend with your partner to discuss and communicate concerns, fears, changes and the impact on your relationship. Donald found this useful, 'We had to re assess how we communicate with each other . . .'

• You may get to a stage when you realise your relationship is not right for you. You might like to consider how and where you can seek support to help you through this. Jules found just this, 'I was no longer able to put up with some of my partner's behaviour. As a result I split up with him and have no regrets.'

• Counselling training may cement and solidify the relationship with your partner. Diana spoke of the 'profound impact' on her relationship where she and her partner were 'increasingly spending more time together, talking more freely about [themselves]'. Similarly, Andrea was able to take on even more, 'We were able to use quite a lot of the counselling framework to share our feelings, thoughts and wishes with each other'.

• Pauline highlights an interesting point in her contribution, referring to the fact that she now talks *with* her partner instead of *to* him.

points to ponder

14
family
dynamics

The term 'family dynamics' refers to the way we interact as a member of a family unit — parents, siblings, children etc. There are clearly links between this chapter and the previous one — both involve the management of relationships. If we are in a close-knit family, where much is shared and aired, then changes in us will be noticed by others. What can be interesting, to say the least, is to note how this impacts on the family group or unit. We have all developed roles and positions within a family and to some extent we feed off the behaviour of other family members.

As we learn more about ourselves during training, different values and behaviours can become more important and this might include how we interact with and within our families. It may be that we no longer want a particular person to make the decisions — we may decide that we would like to have more of a say in decisions. A change and challenge to the norm might then occur as we try to alter what has gone before, and this is where friction may occur.

Another brief account of the effect of counsellor training on the family of the trainee is given in *Step in to Study Counselling* by Pete Sanders, pages 41–43. Full details of the book can be found in Appendix 2.

During training, we are increasingly attempting to understand and integrate the core conditions of empathy, congruence and acceptance. As our level of self-awareness increases, we become more able to choose to adopt the core conditions into our way of living. This may also apply to our family. So by understanding ourselves better, we can feel more open in relating to our family and it may become clearer to us why we respond in a particular way to a specific family member or situation.

During her training, Laura began to see her family as individuals rather than as a unit. She also tried to leave history in the past and relate to each family member as they appeared to her now.

Some believe there is a responsibility on us as trainee counsellors to ease any transition or change in family relationships by offering understanding and clarification. Rick remembers a particular 'discussion' with his father. He had decided, at some length, to make the career change into counselling. Yet when he shared this with his family it came across as a statement, a *fâit accompli*, rather than a family discussion in which he explained his motives, commitment and enthusiasm. His father felt it had came totally out of the blue and was an ill-considered move. The atmosphere was one of defensiveness and stubbornness possibly because of the manner in which Rick had presented the career change, rather than the issue itself.

On other occasions, Rick was heartened to hear feedback from his family in terms of how counselling training contributed to changes in him. The changes highlighted by his immediate family tended to support his view of his own personal development. Such characteristics included — being less stressed and calmer, more mature and worldly, more open and challenging, able to value people more and be less critical, less judgemental and less opinionated. He was slightly disappointed to hear he was perceived as being less opinionated! There is nothing wrong with having an opinion but perhaps what is important is how this is communicated to others.

We were interested to note that despite the large number of contributors who responded to the request for case-studies for other topics, very few added material for this particular chapter. Perhaps contributors found that family issues did not cause any real or significant upset or change, at least to the extent that they felt they were not worth writing about.

Sally

My mother's comments on changes she has seen in me are that I have become more calm and gentle in my way of behaving and more aware of the effect I can have on other people. I have clearer boundaries and expectations in my relationships and I let people know about them.

My older sister finds that I am much happier than before, more peaceful inside, more patient and a more mature person. She is a practitioner of complementary medicine and she has grown to value counselling for both herself and her 'patients'.

My younger sister finds that I have gained a better understanding of myself that allows me to communicate my feelings and thoughts more clearly and that I make use of my personal learnings in the best possible way for myself and for others.

Last but not least, my father, whose comments I don't know, has financially supported my three-year training.

Gary

I'm still getting over my anger. I've been either suppressing or repressing this all my life. My anger vented first during a skills practice session. I was the pretend counsellor and my friend Helen was the pretend client. Quite innocently she spoke of an issue, which as far as I know was a made-up scenario, but it involved being locked in a bedroom when she was young, each time she was 'naughty'. This was a trigger for my torrent of past anguish based on how my father would push me into the hall cupboard when I was very young, simply because I made too much noise. I painfully remember whimpering away for hours in the claustrophobic space. I still hate my father, I think he was evil, a real hard bastard. I have difficulty forgiving him and I can honestly say that I look forward to the freeing presence I expect to feel when he dies. I have not spoken to him for 15 years and don't think I ever will. But despite the anger, the anguish and the memories, I am starting to explore the concept of forgiveness, more for my sake than his. I would never have contemplated this before my course.

Margo   During my counselling training I felt connected to a family of people who, like me, were training in counselling. This extended family taught me the value of my immediate family. Rather than trying to build a new one, I spent time renewing my relationships with my husband and sons. I think they thought I was a bit crazy at times. I revelled in trying to be very un-British, being impulsive, expressive and very open. This was fun. And it rubbed off on everyone. We all became closer . . . and more open. One of the funniest sights for me in recent years was when we all went boating at the local lake. Henry, my husband, a rather traditional university senior lecturer, stood up in the boat and pitching at the top of his voice started to serenade me and the boys. How I love spontaneity.

The newly acquired values have helped a lot in relationships within my family, both in the area of clearer, less tangled communications and with my daughter who was a very truculent adolescent. Their deeper integration within me helped me to accept her and still value and respect her, as well as love her.   *Caroline*

Tammy   I was not really aware of huge changes except I am more able to let others do their own thing and not get drawn into patterns of behaviour that I used to. I suppose that means my boundaries are better defined but also include a bit of disengagement. I still find certain things difficult but I am more able to express my feelings so my behaviour is less misunderstood.

I find my family has become closer, even though my parents worked in the helping professions anyway. My younger sister (my only other sibling) and I get on better. I find it funny that I am happy to be exceptionally juvenile with her at times, horsing about, making faces etc., partly because I now feel free to express much more of me and not be constrained by any parental conditions of worth, i.e. how I should behave! It is also great fun acting like a seven year-old at times . . . you should try it!   *Robin*

George   I became a stranger to my family, they dare not speak to me. I was isolated within the domestic family and welcomed by a larger family. My peers grew together. *I became myself.* This self had a dramatic effect on the life that I had lived.

     My family wished not to speak. Home was hostile. Suddenly no one wanted to have a choice, suddenly I was making a choice for me, suddenly I was being myself and hearing the people around me and sharing what I had heard. No one liked what I heard them say. Suddenly they were being challenged to account for their actions and sayings instead of me tolerating and doing for them. Those family members do not know me, thay have chosen to stay in their safe place.

I find I have become aware of a double-edged sword with regards to my family. On the one hand I am more tolerant of the various squabbles and disagreements which crop up now and again yet, on the other hand I'm also more aware of them . . . I see them more but I'm more tolerant? I also want to intervene when in the past I wouldn't. My mother, for instance, has always been a bit of a nagger, especially to my father. But I dislike seeing this. It pains me. Once I asked my mother to stop nagging my father. I don't think it ever had entered her mind that   *David* she was actually 'nagging'. At first she just laughed this off, then got defensive. I don't know if my words really helped?

> ***Pundeep*** I moved away from my parents and to some extent much of my culture about seven years ago. This was a conscious effort to release myself from the family chains of expectations. It was tough breaking away and I spent several years feeling like I didn't fit in, which was very tough indeed. I feel that my counselling training has opened my eyes more about the effect of family dynamics and the huge power that exists there. Potentially the time bomb ticks away until that's it. We're never taught how to get along with our family and why should we respect our elders if we do not respect them? Catch 22.

points to ponder

• Discuss your interest and enthusiasm about counselling, if you can, with your family before and during training, especially during or after significant workshops.

• Prepare your family, if you can, for what you are about to embark on.

• Let your family read this book but be prepared for questions!

• You may encounter difficulties with your family as a result of changes to you during training. Family dynamics exist within a complex set of needs and wants for all of you. A change to you will create a change for someone else. Be prepared to put your new-found counselling skills to the test.

• Your family may trivialise your work. This is most often because they do not understand, rather than from malicious intent. Try not to let this get to you.

• You may feel some resistance in wanting to change your relationship with your family. This may cause you some confusion and difficulty in accepting your part in the family.

• You may discover the process of training offers you the freedom and support to begin to understand your family and their meaning to you.

• Observations about changes to us can be very insightful. Sally's mother felt she had 'become more calm and gentle in [her] way of behaving and more aware of the effect [she could] have on other people'. Her sister went further by saying 'much happier, more peaceful inside, more patient and a more mature person'.

• However, there are examples where the family interaction becomes strained. George's situation shows us the other side, 'I became a stranger to my family, they dare not speak to me. . . Home was hostile'.

• David explains how he found his enhanced self-awareness became a 'double-edged sword'. This might be a response to being more aware and astute but perhaps there are ways in which this can work for us more in a favourable way than not?

• An improvement in relationships can happen.

**15
the impact
on friends
and friend-
ships**

Completing this section on *Interpersonal Relationships*, this chapter covers friendships, how they impact on and influence our training experience and, importantly, vice versa. Again there are similarities between this and the previous three chapters. How we are with our friends has implications for how we relate and communicate with one another on the course. How we respond to the training experience might be influenced by how we previously related to others. For instance, several trainees have found that the new level of intimacy and depth of new friendships from course peers lead them to question the depths of friendships they had before. Retrospectively they feel that previous friendships might have lacked depth, might have been more superficial.

Trainees frequently highlight how they feel isolated from the 'outside world' during counselling training. The intense and intimate training environment can sometimes seem artificial, detached from the real world. Or to look at it from another angle, once a trainee is receiving and offering real and meaningful responses, it can be hard to return to superficial relationships. So when trainees are continually sharing personal and private thoughts and feelings, they are offering very close, intimate support and everyone is in the same boat. This openness and honesty is, perhaps unfortunately, not usual in most everyday relationships. In itself, this can be an illuminating insight and many trainees find that this intimate relationship experienced during training is the way they want to lead their lives in the future and to this extent they complete their training with a mission to live their lives in this more open and intimate manner.

Rick feels he distanced himself from several friends because of this new-found intimacy, but what he learnt through this experience was that he felt he was being extremely judgemental. Another dawning realisation was that perhaps he was also guilty of conspiring to make the friendships 'superficial'. What Rick was able to realise and respond to, was the value of recreating and reinforcing the old friendships with a greater degree of openness to them. The result has been very successful. The friendships are much stronger and both sides are closer and more understanding of the other.

Remember, your friends will not be benefiting from the insights and learnings of counselling training. While you would like all of them to understand precisely what counselling is and why it is so important to you, you cannot expect them to slot into 'understanding' mode.

Laura learnt to openly express her value for her friends. This has increased the strength, depth and fun of these friendships. The training environment can offer a forum to test out a new way of being.

Some trainees will come across friends who want to be counselled. The BAC Code of Ethics [see Appendix 2 for further details] suggests that counselling friends is not ethical and while we, as trainees, may understand this, it can be difficult sometimes to communicate this to friends. However, if troubled friends do make a beeline for us, it would seem practical to have distinct options for a response. Firstly, we can be friends and do what friends do — provide a shoulder to cry on, be a sounding board, support and just listen to them. Maybe it takes practice to differentiate between being a supportive friend and counselling someone, particularly having experienced thorough counselling training. We can help a friend find a counsellor if that's what they want and if they feel this might help. Our link to, and experience of, the profession may encourage them to try this resource which they might not otherwise.

Fi

I encourage my friends and relatives to explore within themselves and rely on their abilities to identify their difficulties and solve their problems. Also I feel other people can be enriched and empowered in my company because I feel enriched and empowered within myself.

Tony

I still find that people have their own impression about counsellors. In fact, I think I probably am guilty of that as well. If I'm in a social situation and am meeting people for the first time, I do evaluate how and what I say to them. I find it different if I say I'm a counsellor to that of being a psychotherapist. In my mind the former sounds more approachable, the latter more professional. So it depends what message I feel best about.

Another thing is that people I meet for the first time get the impression that I am analysing them! I find this very frustrating because I don't. I sometimes think this pulls people back from me, they're resistant, fearing that I have this strange power. I usually try to make a joke when I'm accused of this by saying 'tell me about this concern that I'm analysing you' and throw it back to them!

Emily

I found the intensity of relating to people all day meant I felt extremely unsociable when I got home and in the first term I hardly phoned anyone and did not go out much. The thought of relating to more people was more than I could bear! This has improved a bit though there are still times when I come home weepy and sad due to something which has touched me deeply.

I have always found that I have examined and adjusted my attitudes towards minority groups in society, particularly gays and lesbians and disabled people. Excellent awareness-raising workshops started the process and I have done some reading on my own. I found that I had always considered myself open and accepting but in fact was actually denying *the differences*. I had not thought it important to acknowledge that someone was gay or disabled because I thought it was enough to treat them like *anyone else* — which actually meant like me, heterosexual and not disabled. This was a jolt and an area I am still working on.

Sharon

I've had differing response from my friends. One wanted to use me as a free counsellor. Most of them have just accepted me as I am but I have heard other comments through lesser acquaintances such as: 'you just talk to them, what good can that do?'; 'clients must be weak or failing in life in some way'; 'How is your little practice going then?'; 'Counsellors are a group of non-regulated do-gooders'.

I haven't had any explicit comments from my friends. However, some friends are more inclined to say, 'Oh, yes, I wanted to talk to you about _____ and see what you think'. There is thus an implication that I have some expertise that they want to use or tap into to help verify or validate their experiences/explanations.

In terms of people in general, I have always tried to accept people as they are. I work with minorities and have no problems so far. The most difficult area is with people who think of counselling as being self-indulgent on the part of both counsellor and client.

Rory

I have probably half the number of friends that I had before my training. However those I do have now seem to have been carefully chosen, so their importance and value to me is immense. We have a much closer bond, freed from the superficialities and masochism of some of my earlier relationships.

I was incredibly angry when a female friend of mine said I was a 'big woman' now I was a counsellor. This felt an attack on my maleness, and stereotypified counselling as a comfy, woolly, female thing. It is none of that but can be. It is a profession and a vocation that I am immensely proud and humbled to be part of.

I also find I have settled into a nice habit of thanking the till checkout worker at the supermarket by name. It values and appreciates them as a person rather than a number on a conveyer belt. I like my attention to things like that.

Debbie

I feel that I have a very strong affinity with all my friends and in all my friendships. There is greater meaning and quality of connection. Perhaps I have learnt a new dimension of love because this is what it feels like, a kind of love. It almost feels like all my stakes have been raised, proportionately. The depth of love I used to feel with my partner is now the level I feel with my friends, a real soulful love. My partner gets even more from me now but it's my friends who probably notice more. I love them and I'm in love with them as my friends. My partner has a more intimate depth from me but he does not have exclusivity for who I am. Many of my friends are able to tap into my attractiveness and love for them.

Alison

I find that my counselling training has illuminated a very sobering point with regards to friendships and that is the many I have just let go over time. I've had great and special friends at the various stages of my life but many have just drifted away. This is probably a mutual thing but that can be an excuse. I don't know where half of these people are now. But it makes me focus more effort, attention and commitment to the current friendships I have.

Michael   I've always been pretty sociable but something has changed since my counselling training and this is a good space to tentatively explore this. I now have a strong base of friends, all of whom are very supportive for each other. But there is also something about how strong the friendships are. I know in my circle of some seven really close friends, we'd do anything for each other. I feel honoured to have this. It feels very special. I'd be interested to find out where this comes from. Perhaps I put more into the value of friendships now or am I more open, honest and approachable? Or have I just coincidentally met a really special bunch of people. I suppose I'm trying to work out whether there is something in me that has changed to be receptive to this group . . . and if so, I'll bottle it and make a fortune!

points to ponder

- It might help to speak with your friends before you start training and explain what you are going to do and why.

- Some friends, like the public, may be sceptical and suspicious of counselling. Sharon's 'lesser acquaintances' belittled her work, 'you just talk to them, what good can that do?' and 'counsellors are a group of non-regulated do-gooders'.

- You may make new friends during your counselling training.

- You may come to the conclusion that some of your 'old' friendships are not worth hanging on to. This may cause some confusion for yourself and friends. It may be hard for friends to accept the pace of your development. You may also discover new depths in 'old' friendships. Friends may be able to share different parts of themselves with you, now that you have changed.

- You may finish training with a stronger appreciation of friendships and the sorts of people you would like to have as friends in the future. As Rory states, this can focus on the quality rather than quantity of friendships: 'I have probably half the number of friends that I had before my training . . . [but] their importance and value to me is immense. We have a much closer bond, freed from the superficialities and masochism of some of my earlier relationships.'

- Counselling training may encourage you to reflect on the values attached to friendships past and present. Alison tells us of the friends who she has lost touch with, those who have 'just drifted away'. Working at a sustained depth with our peers may provide us with new breadth and depths of friendships.

This penultimate section attempts to cover the eight most significant operational or structural aspects of the training experience. It reflects the framework within which personal and professional development occur. It raises points which may help you decide on the level, degree of structure, length, delivery and format of training you may prefer to choose.

Every counselling training experience is different. The syllabus may be comparable between several training centres but the way in which the course is administered, managed, implemented and delivered is where the variety occurs. Courses, within the person-centred 'stable', are most significantly differentiated because of, and by, the people who run them. If you are at the stage of deciding to start training, you may find the case-study experiences will perhaps both answer some of your questions and also provoke more questions. In true person-centred style, the book hopes to guide and support a person's self-questioning so that the individual can seek out, and find, their own answers.

The most direct way to find out about particular courses — their content and way of working — is to find people who have been on a particular course before and ask them what it was like. You must bear in mind that they will be giving you their impressions. They will be *personal*, not *objective* and one person's likes will be another person's dislikes.

In Section C, under professional development, the responses point to the influential role staff or tutors had on a trainee's development. Chapter 16 provides an insight into what some trainers, tutors or staff have contributed to the training experience, through the eyes of the trainee. It is interesting to hear how some former trainees rate the staff (generally very positively) and, as ever, the range of contributions represents an even sway of opinion.

Modes, structures and levels of training receive attention in Chapter 17 and this will give you an idea of the academic and experiential demands at different levels. Constraints on funding (see Chapter 18 and Appendix 1) may necessitate local study and so the availability and standard of local training will dictate what course you can apply for. Furthermore, entry to counselling training usually begins with some introduction or counselling skills course and so this may shape your route into training.

Application and recruitment was a topic area which was listed originally to encourage feedback from contributors but there was a surprisingly small number of people who had any opinion, feelings or views on this. Surprising, that is, because getting selected onto a course can be a tense affair. Perhaps, in retrospect, few people commented on this section because those who did contribute were successfully invited to attend a course. The issue of failing a selection process did not occur for them. This omission is acknowledged.

Funding is one of the greatest concerns for trainees, before, during and after training. It can be an expensive education. Chapter 18 shows us how several trainees dealt with the issue of money and may help you reflect on financial factors which you will need to take into account. Since much tertiary, further or vocational training is becoming self-funding, the vast majority of courses do not have any official funding structure and so trainees are required to fund themselves. The testimonies in this chapter may offer a few ideas where funding might be sought but, obviously, there are no guarantees. Some trainees may be eligible to claim tax relief on the cost of course fees though the criteria will not be applicable to everyone.

Sometimes a company may actively support and encourage certain staff to train in counselling/counselling skills and as such may be open to paying fees, an allowance or at least a contribution towards costs. Several, however, may well issue a clause with any such funding which would request a recipient to repay the monies if they leave the company within a specified time, i.e. this could become what is known as a 'golden handcuff' — a benefit which locks you in!

Summative assessment is assessment that occurs at the end of a course, traditionally an exam or project or disseration (a very long essay). In traditional education, this kind of assessment os marked by the tutors.

Self and peer assessment are usual components of person-centred training. It may sound strange to many readers, familiar only with traditional, authority-based tutor assessed education. Discovering how *you* get on with self and peer assessment is an important part of personal and professional development in person-centred training.

Chapter 19 asks former trainees how person-centred their training was. This counselling approach encourages empowerment, self-responsibility, genuineness, empathy and unconditional positive regard. But to what extent is this emulated by the structure and delivery of, for instance, the course work, or the feedback from staff, or the openness of workshops, lectures, seminars etc? A course is not forced to be person-centred but if included in the course description it should be reflected in the spirit of the training. It would seem consistent and perhaps obvious that a course claiming to teach a specific style or approach should be faithful to the approach in its content and method. The case-studies illustrate the range of opinion felt on whether courses were person-centred and how important this was to trainees.

A key part of this type of training relates to self-assessment as a means of measuring and monitoring our professional development. Most of us will be used to more formalised summative tutor-assessment. But in person-centred training we may be more encouraged to evaluate ourselves. The honesty and openness generated by self-assessment can sometimes confound the critics who claim self-assessment is open to abuse. The benefit of self-assessment is to initiate in the counsellor the skill of self-reflection, self-evaluation, self-monitoring. Chapter 20 looks at how trainees experienced the particular assessment methods used on their course.

The end of a course can be an emotional experience of transition, as former trainees explain in Chapter 21. This can be an emotional time for a number of reasons. In a good training experience, a trainee will have bonded with a fairly large group of probably very diverse individuals, sharing and struggling through a journey of self-discovery with designs to advance their counselling skills. There may have been ups and downs, times of frustration and boredom, and times of elation and depression but it may have been possible to share this. The intimacy and intensity felt by the close bonding and sharing may well have touched everyone quite deeply, and the participants will soon be re-entering the real world where things will be different.

Having finished a training course, trainees often come away with clear suggestions on how the training experience might be improved. A number of ideas are quoted in Chapter 22. There are relatively few contributions for this chapter. One reason may be that most courses will have an 'evaluation' questionnaire which is given to trainees as they complete training. This will ask for comments on the course and provide an opportunity to give an opinion on things to do better, i.e. how that particular course might improve for future trainees. It is difficult to say to what extent such advice, suggestions or opinions are taken on board.

Chapter 23, at the end of this section, features feedback which summarises what it is like *to be person-centred* as a result of the training. Is it a *way of being* only within the therapeutic relationship? There is an obvious connection here between this chapter and Chapter 19, 'How person-centred was my course?' These have been separated to prevent confusion because they do refer to quite different issues, one about the external (Chapter 19) and the other the internal (Chapter 23) — the personal feeling of 'being' person-centred in a world that is often experienced as hostile to person-centred values and attitudes.

16
tutors

It is desirable, some would say essential, that *core* tutors on person-centred counselling courses should have qualifications in *person-centred* or *client-centred* counselling. Failing that, they should be able to show how their continuing professional development has included a substantial involvement in person-centred events.

Another good sign is that tutors are members of BAPCA, PCT Scotland, ADPCA (Association for the Development of the Person-Centered Approach) or a similar organisation dedicated to person-centred or client-centred development.

Tutors can also be accredited as trainers by BAC. It means that they are experienced trainers and have demonstrated their competence at various levels of training. They can use the letters BAC Acc Tr after their name.

For simplicity, trainers, course staff, tutors and facilitators will be hereafter referred to as 'tutors'.

The tutor's role during training is crucial, as it is in any teaching relationship. Many of us will have shone at school/university in subjects where we most connected with a particular tutor, who we understood, respected and whose style we enjoyed. Our previous personal experience of education can impact on our feelings towards the tutors and the course, so it can be helpful to be aware of these feelings.

Laura felt extremely nervous on the first day of the course. It was based in a university, and she was aware of wanting to be 'good' and get everything right. She realised that this came from how she'd felt at school. The building her course was housed in was a similar environment to a large school. Since the university also ran educational psychology and teaching courses, one floor of the building exhibited children's artwork. The combination of these elements triggered memories of being back at school. She found it helped to acknowledge these feelings and move on without tainting the current experience.

Often tutors are involved in a dual role. They may have a responsibility to the overall administration and managing of the course and, at the same time, they can have a personal involvement in the course through the experiential quality of most counselling courses. It may be difficult, initially, to relate to an individual in both roles. Generally, the tutor-related experiences of most contributors shared with us have been very positive. However, there will inevitably be some tutors who people just do not get on with.

Rick became wary of one particular tutor during a part of his training. He felt the trainer was very 'picky' in the sense that nothing that Rick said escaped enquiry or questioning. Initially, Rick became very defensive about this, preferring to sit out meetings with this tutor in silence. But it became evident to Rick that it wasn't that he disliked the tutor, but rather that he was not used to the focused attention and challenging. What he soon realised was that he was anxious about saying what he felt, instinctively and spontaneously, and it was this perceived calculatedness in Rick that the tutor was challenging. Rick's defensive attitude slowly evaporated as he risked being spontaneous, content to deal with his responses as and when they came out. Out of a seemingly fraught trainee/tutor relationship came a real insight.

Laura found it extremely useful to meet with the course tutors prior to applying for the course. It helped her to grasp the range of counselling and academic experience within their team. It was important for her that the course was experiential. However, she also required a rigorous academic background in order to help her understand the philosophy underpinning the experiential work.

Challenge can be a vital part of learning where the insightful observations of tutors (and, of course, our peers) can shed light on some hidden issues for us. Tutors are only human and, like the best of counsellors, are prone to mistakes, frustrations and errors of judgement, and then again, trainees might marvel at the skills, intuition and awareness of tutors. Frequently, trainees measure their development against tutors and while this can be a useful yardstick it can also be quite unrealistic. How can a trainee, with five months training and minimal client work, compete with (for example) the 15-year experience of a tutor, having taught for five years, seen many hundreds of clients in several work contexts.

Some tutors on person-centred courses appear to be exceptionally person-centred (covered in more depth in Chapters 19 and 23) but there are courses which feature a range of tutors with different backgrounds and using different counselling approaches. This can provide some very useful diversity. Practising person-centred therapists can work in different ways and do not necessarily agree on all issues — providing an interesting area of debate during training and a fruitful way to develop our own views and way of working.

Much of counselling training is experiential — we learn through our experience. Although a workshop may be planned on a specific topic, the timetable will be left open-ended to take account of the desires and learning needs of the group; because of this there will be a certain degree of unpredictability.

It has not been unknown for tutors to disagree with each other quite strongly. Some might claim this is unprofessional. Others might say this is being person-centred. Rick was aware of one case when this happened at a particular workshop. It was fascinating to witness how the anger that crept in was so quickly defused by both tutors. They stepped back from their personal stances and brought in a dialogue with the other, seeking awareness, offering reason, logic and positive feelings. It was a wonderful experience as it showed him, and no doubt other trainees, not just how easily an argument can occur but more importantly how this can be profitably dealt with. This was a real-life experience and one which brought reality to the training much more than books, videos or lectures could ever have done.

Although the sidenote on the previous page makes the point that *core* tutors should preferably have a good background in the person-centred approach, many courses involve tutors trained in other theoretical approaches to provide input specifically on those approaches.

It is probably not a good idea, though, to have a course team (on a person-centred course) made up from tutors none of whom have been trained specifically in the person-centred approach. Such practice can give rise to the idea that anyone can run person-centred training, and this is, of course vigorously challenged by bodies such as BAPCA.

Suzy   I felt that the Head of the course was a very mature, experienced and well-rounded person who always offered the 'Core Conditions' to us, although he never let us get away with denial or incongruence. His teaching style was clear and easy to listen to and understand. He was also my Personal Development Group Facilitator and, although I knew he also had an assessor's role, it says a lot about his experience in that I still felt safe in that group. However, where I do feel that we, as course members, were disadvantaged, was in two of the Skills Groups. These particular groups had two inexperienced facilitators who were not very good at holding the groups, encouraging the groups or making them feel safe in what is, after all ,quite a difficult part of the course. We were all feeling deskilled and disadvantaged to some degree.

I also experienced my Personal Tutor as unsupportive. At that time I definitely needed support as I was not at all confident academically. The main difficulty for me with regard to his input was that he always seemed to find several things wrong with my assignment which, when I did the next one, I would seek to address. Then he would find several more things wrong with the next one. There was never an acknowledgement of the areas I had addressed, nor encouragement, and it always left me feeling that nothing was ever good enough.

The facilitators were genuine, real in the true sense of the word, the 'conditions'   ***Don***
were there to be witnessed.

     Caroline   Sometimes feedback from the staff is not clear as they are so keen that we work things out ourselves and do not just get fed the answers (which I appreciate) but, at the same time, sometimes more clarity would have been welcomed.

My experience of the trainers has been very positive. I feel they set an excellent example as person-centred counsellors for trainees to base themselves on. They have been accessible and open, always challenging me but there to pick up the pieces as well. I have found them very responsible in all the workshops that have been run. Their enthusiasm comes across but, at the same time, I have really appreciated their discipline around time boundaries and the way care is taken that everyone receives a fair amount of time and workshops and so on start and finish punctually. (I previously worked in an organisation where time was not valued at all so it is a refreshing change!)

I have been able to communicate my feelings towards one trainer where I felt I disagreed with her on issues, and that was received very positively. The trainers for supervision and personal development have been very facilitative and taken care of me in the groups. The trainers are very open and are always quick to take responsibility for how they are feeling about a response or a challenge from the trainees.

I feel the course was very well run and the experience and enthusiasm of the   *Evelyn*
trainers was apparent. I felt that on a couple of occasions there was a bit of conflict between two of the three trainers. One was the course deputy and far more an advocate of Rogers than the others. This seemed to cause a great deal of anxiety for some of the students but it did not really seem to affect me — probably because I felt that they were the experts and thus well equipped to sort out their own problems. Also perhaps I am less worried by conflict than some other students. I remember thinking that there was probably a lot of transference going on; students seeing their trainers as their quarrelling parents — and then being surprised that *I was thinking like a counsellor!*

Rosie   I found there was some lack of judgement by one particular tutor. There was poor communication with regards to the aims and objectives, particularly of group work. There was concern about confidentiality in counselling exercises between students of different years and tutors/supervisors. As the issue of confidentiality was not made explicit in the counselling sessions we were left to make our own sense and interpretation.

Looking back over the three years, it seems to have taken a long time to acquire the attitudes, values and beliefs within person-centred counselling. In terms of the trainers, although most of the time they also espoused those values, sometimes their own attitudes were delivered as being *right*. The trainers are invested with more power than either party realises and the delivery of such attitudes can be powerful. However, generally the power of this phantasy lessens as the trainee comes to realise that the trainer is just another person and not *perfect* as the trainee may be phantasising they should be.

I also found that some trainers adopted very dogmatic interpretations of famous psychologists and therapists, which did not always match my understanding of their work.

The delivery and contact of workshops and lectures has always made them useful. I find that it is up to me to get something out of it although the 'something' can be impossible to predict and sometimes difficult to define.

I have an ongoing transferential situation with one of my tutors. I know that, in pure Rogerian terms transference is not part of the picture, but I know that I am treating my tutor like one of my parents from time to time and this makes it very difficult to see her as herself. However, we are able to discuss this and I can reflect on this. This has led me to understand myself, my relationship with that parent and how transferred feelings can distort my perception. One has to be careful not to overcompensate though and dismiss all feelings as being transferred. The emphasis may change and some of my feelings are quite understandable if someone behaves in certain ways to me.

The ability of my tutors to blend theory with practice has generally been excellent with just the occasional difficulty. But I think this is more because the group is quite large (19) and there really is not time for everyone to have their say all the time, particularly regarding theoretical issues.

Carol

While most, if not all, of the trainers were undoubtedly skilled, knowledgeable and sensitive companions of warm and honest challenge to me, they were also inconsistent with the underlying philosophy of the Person-Centred Approach. They would combine different ways from other humanistic approaches that proceed from quite different assumptions and traditions. It demanded great effort on my part, and certainly time, to realise the effects of this on my work.

Carl   The tutors were very committed to the course, very knowledgeable in their field and extremely enthusiastic.

I found my tutors supportive and informative and was able to work through my   *Jenny*
need to please authority in my first year because my tutor was so willing and open
to my challenge — and supportive of me whilst I did it!

Rodge   I felt all my tutors were excellent in at least one role they took on, but interestingly
I could fault each one for perhaps taking too much on or working in an area where
they had less experience. By the end of a full-time Diploma, I became aware of
alliances that were taking place between students and tutors. There were some
quite tense clashes at the end and what was unfortunate about these was not that
they took place (for I found such incidences hugely invaluable 'in the moment'
exchanges) but that they were not aired as openly as they could have been. I
would also like to point out that I feel it is the ultimate challenge to be a tutor,
facilitator or member of staff on a person-centred course. I have a huge amount of
respect for them and cannot fault their dedication, commitment and willingness to
learn as well.

points to ponder

- Tutors, like you, are only human and are likely to make mistakes at times.

- If you are aware of a personality clash with a tutor or feel someone 'has it in
for you' discuss this with them, highlighting your concerns, and if this is
not remedied speak to another staff member requesting confidentiality from
the outset.

- Be aware of how you are responding to staff members. Do you treat him/her
as an authority figure? If so, why? Do you react to anyone else in this way?
If yes, are you able to start understanding why? To what extent are you
contributing to this situation?

- Don't be afraid to challenge and confront a tutor. An important part of your
learning and development within a person-centred course is your interaction
with the other group members. A tutor is a group member and will participate
in their own way. You are at liberty to challenge, confront, explore, share
with a tutor in the way you would with a fellow trainee.

- Different tutors (and different courses) prefer more or less rigid roles for
staff. It will help avoid misunderstandings if you find out where they —
and you — stand. Caroline, for example, experienced confusion: 'Sometimes
feedback from the staff is not clear as they are so keen that we work things
out ourselves . . . at the same time sometimes more clarity would have been
welcomed'.

- The range of skills, experience and competences will vary between courses
and institutions. For Carl, his tutors were 'very committed to the course,
very knowledgeable in their field and extremely enthusiastic'. Likewise,

Jenny found her tutors 'supportive and informative'. But this was not the experience of everyone. Carol found her tutors as being, ' . . . inconsistent with the underlying philosophy of the Person-Centred Approach.' and Jeremy felt his 'tutors were . . . in a place of judgement'.

• Rodge seems to offer a poignant remark in his offering by suggesting it is the 'ultimate challenge' to be a tutor! Perhaps tutors have something to say about this?

experi-ences of

person-centred counselling training

17

modes and structures of training

Although employers might be impressed by qualifications *per se*, it might be better to find out how many hours of training there are on the course (this figure should exclude placement hours). In general — although there *will* be variations in this — part-time courses fall into three levels: 1. introductory (evening classes lasting 10-12 weeks)[20–30 hours]; 2. certifcate or intermediate (evening classes lasting one academic year)[100–150 hours]; 3. diploma or professional (day/ evening classes lasting two academic years)[300–500 hours].

The BAC runs schemes to accredit individual counsellors, trainers and supervisors, and a scheme to accredit courses, working a bit

This is a difficult chapter to introduce since there is a huge variety of courses currently offering counselling, or counselling skills training, with many different qualifications. This makes it practically impossible to present a clear and accurate overview of counsellor training.

The myriad of levels include Certificates, Advanced Certificates, National Vocational Qualifications (NVQs), Scottish Vocational Qualications (SVQs), Diplomas, Advanced Diplomas, Person-Centred Diplomas, first degrees (BA, BSc) and higher degrees (MA, MSc, PhD) etc. A specific course in one college or institute offering one level will be different from another offering the same. Differences may include depth and breadth of topic, amount and type of theory, written assignments, practice, placement requirements and personal counselling requirements.

There may be further discrepancies due to the location of courses. The further and higher education systems of Scotland differ from that of England, Wales and Northern Ireland in admissions criteria, level of qualification and length of study. This may well impact on counselling courses too.

In some regions there will be part-time courses and full-time courses offered, but this is not the case countrywide. A decision to choose a part- or full-time course may be determined, in part, by funding, ability to take time off work, access and availability. The profession as a whole does not seem to favour one over the other, so the choice really is yours depending upon your needs and your means. Part-time courses generally run for longer periods than full-time courses, at the same academic levels. Part-time courses may provide a longer period of time for reflection, development and growth. However, full-time courses may facilitate a greater intensity, albeit over a shorter period of time. Much will therefore depend on individual preferences.

In addition to 'on-campus' training, at a university, college or training centre, there are also some organisations offering correspondence courses. These tend not to include any face-to-face contact and so may provide little or no scope for developing skills, attitudes and practice in a setting with other people. Correspondence courses will provide access to training for many who cannot travel to 'on-campus' courses. It may be worth taking advice before investing in such distance-learning training, since person-centred counselling relies heavily on learning through experience and this simply may not be possible in a distance-learning model. It may also be the case that professional bodies might not recognise such training for membership or accreditation purposes.

The diversity of training courses available is not necessarily a fault of the counselling profession, nor is it limited to person-centred training. Counselling courses may operate different assessment methods to more formal academic courses and so there can be a difficulty in fitting such course criteria into a university or college academic framework.

There is one measure which may provide some degree of commonality and this relates to courses accredited by the BAC. Accreditation of your training course may be important to future employers, however, there will be many other excellent training opportunities where training providers do not have this accreditation.

like a 'kite-mark' of quality. A BAC Accredited course will have been thoroughly scrutinised — staff, accommodation, the training hours devoted to theory, personal development and practice development, integrity of the curriculum, and how it is delivered. There is more on course accreditation in the sidenores on pages 16 and 63.

Susanna

The skills learning on the Diploma was different from that on the MSc. The latter seems to be much more about the skills of debate, self-directed learning, negotiation and analysis than any practical skills. The experience of the development of the said skills is probably the main reason I feel correspondence courses, particularly in counselling anyway, would not be an effective way to learn, even with the contact times some of these courses have. The contact times seem to be quite infrequent and the courses as a whole do not seem to provide the same facility for relationship-building and self-awareness development as other types of experiential courses, not to mention the lack of opportunity for debate and discussion.

The course was supposed to be part-time but in practice once on the Certificate stage, and certainly by the Diploma stage, the course took over my whole life. Those who were working full-time with one day-release from work found that every evening of their week was taken up with either client work, co-counselling or assignment preparation.

Jenny

Gary

I took the year full-time Diploma and found almost every waking hour consumed by the course in some way or another. It made me realise how important it was to look after myself and know when to step back from the action when necessary. I had had a very traumatic client experience shortly before our residential weekend and whilst many of the workshops and guest speakers were really fascinating, I spent much of the time going on walks and being apart from the set-up. It was important to do this as a way to take care of myself — to give myself space.

I met several people who had studied on the two-year part-time course and we reflected on our respective experiences. We concluded that I got the complete immersion and intensity, whereas they got the more longer-term processing of skills. We could not identify any significant strength or weakness for either mode and put this down to what suited the individual in terms of funding, work commitments and general preference.

One of my sisters is currently doing an MA in Counselling on a correspondence course which does not involve any contact with clients at all! I have had to try and

Jan

distinguish between the two courses, as my parents and other sisters are confused why mine is a Diploma and hers an MA!

The full-time course was the only option for me as I felt I needed the concentration of time to get into the work. I was fortunate in having a partner who was working (on and off!) and had also saved up funds.

> *Nigel*
>
> In the four years of my training, two I spent learning to counsel-by-numbers: 'Here a paraphrase, there a paraphrase, everywhere a paraphrase. Old MacDonald was a shrink . . .' For two years I was on a course which gave a philosophy to my experience as client and as a human being and enabled me to find the tools (intellectual and skilled) to live well, to become alive and then to counsel. I brought words, pictures, movements, my experiences of being a person, or becoming a person and not letting go of that gift. And then I learned how they might be used to walk with others as they stumble to another version of their reality.
>
> And we began to integrate our many levels of learning and experience. I suddenly found that the theory that I had gained through loving music and art and dance really could resonate within the counselling process. And the playful — delightful, like a cat chasing a tail of string.

Sally

I chose a part-time route to fit in with work. The course was a Certificate in Professional Counselling though I don't know how this compares with other courses either at Certificate or Diploma level. In my experience, I would say that experientially this is at the Diploma level or perhaps higher, whilst theoretically perhaps at the Certificate level.

There has been very little information with regards to further or advanced study courses. I did want to progress to do my Postgraduate Diploma in Counselling Psychology with the official governing body but at present cannot afford to do this. I hope to continue in my current job and work towards BAC Accreditation and thereafter work towards becoming a Chartered Counselling Psychologist.

I do not think it is possible to do counselling training like this by distance learning. It is through the opportunity to interrelate to different people in specific settings and in group work and being challenged that enables you to fully realise how you may appear to others, notice your blind spots, defences, phantasies etc. By correspondence you may only deal with what you want to deal with because there is no forum where you can be effectively challenged.

With regards to the conflict of work and study, I found that fine, hence why I chose the part-time course. I personally liked having the week to do things to allow insights to process and to not be permanently introspective to the point of not being able to live. Little and often over the three years seems right to me. The process of training cannot be hurried and it does seem to take a long time to fully integrate and absorb into one's personal experience. This is, I feel, due to the 'sorting out' one has to do to know what is your own stuff, what is the client's (if you can tell the difference) and to be able to make things known if you are not sure, i.e. by being transparent with the client, and, if you feel tearful but don't know why, then sharing this with the client in a neutral way. However, if I spent all week working like this I think I would find it difficult to function normally outside the training group.

Hazel   I feel that a full-time course would be a very interesting experience but it has never been an option for me because of home and family commitments. Part-time courses can also be difficult from the perspective of balancing course commitments with family and work. It is fortunate, I feel, especially when I hear about other people's experiences, that I am a naturally focused and organised person.

I therefore did not have too much difficulty in deciding to do my present Master's course. This was also helped by the fact that I have a very understanding and supportive partner who takes the time commitment and personal changes which I experience as a result of being a student, all in his stride. This decision was also motivated by the fact that I see the next stage in my professional development is towards doing more as a Trainer.

Tony

Choosing my course involved weighing up a Diploma or Masters programme, which would be influenced by geographical location and resultant academic credibility which was important as my employer was providing unpaid leave for this period of study. But beyond this there was the major issue of teaching formats — personal development within training and/or developing understanding and knowledge of theory — experiential learning versus book learning. Some person-centred training courses place differing emphasis on these key issues.

I chose a particular Masters programme which suited my needs and beliefs. However, there was a lot of pressure to reach an acceptable academic standard, from what was perceived to be a critical university authority. Examinations were on a range of theoretical topics. The department wished to make the process a significant learning experience around a person-centred approach. How to do both the shared learning and theoretical-based assessments within the year faced students with individual choices and no time for a consensual approach or real opportunity to share broadly. Because people were coming from a number of different counselling frameworks, there was a dramatic change in process after the first term. The first term allowed time for the group to share, come together and establish ourselves in designated tutorial/home groups. This was over just two months, but with many people having other commitments, there was a shortage of quality time. Therefore issues were raised and experiences shared without time to allow these to be developed and deeper insights gained. This was especially so of potential conflict and interpersonal difficulties.

points to ponder

- Are you aware of the requirements of a counselling course, experientially and academically?

- Can you handle these? If so, would it make more sense for you to complete training in an intensive full-time course, or a more spread-out part-time course?

- What prior experience do you have of learning or schooling and how does this influence your preparedness for the counselling course? Nigel, for example, shows us how his creativity became a major strength, 'I suddenly found that the theory that I had gained through loving music and art and dance really could resonate within the counselling process'.

- If you choose a part-time course because you need to continue with a job, can you correctly anticipate the extent of time you will need to commit to the course? Jenny found it difficult to estimate how much time it would take up before the event: 'The course was supposed to be part-time but in practice . . . the course took over my whole life'. But Sally, on the other hand, was OK with this, 'with regards to the conflict of work and study, I found that fine, hence why I chose the part-time course'.

- If funding is less of an issue, would you prefer the intensity of a full-time course over a short period of time or a more sustained and spread-out process of training?

- There is no quick or 'fast-track' way into counselling. Perhaps full-time courses will speed up training time-wise when compared with part-time study. During training, many trainees realise that becoming a proficient counsellor is not about getting through training as quickly as possible. In person-centred training, much of the development that goes on for us is internal, i.e. within us. It is how we take on board new insights, how we improve our emotional self-awareness, how we develop an emotional intelligence. This takes time to filter through into practice.

- If you are interested in pursuing further academic study after your counselling course, have you considered your motivations behind this?

- Consider what degree of skills practice, group interaction, feedback processes and learning feels appropriate for you, particularly on courses which do not feature skills practice or are run by correspondence. As Susanna points out, 'The experience of the development of [debate, self-directed learning, negotiation and analysis] is probably the main reason I feel correspondence courses, particularly in counselling, would not be an effective way to learn'. Sally seconds this point, 'I do not think it is possible to do counselling training . . . by distance learning'.

18
funding

The issue of funding is one of the greatest determinants of where, how and when you embark on training. Counselling training is a hugely expensive exercise and one which appears to be disqualified from most government, national and regional education grants. Trainees fund themselves in a variety of ways. Some will have spent a number of years saving for the training — if you bear in mind course fees, ancillary course costs, living and accommodation expenses, then it can add up to a tidy sum. Much clearly depends on the type of course you choose and someone who picks a full-time course located further than a commutable distance away from home will need more funding than someone living at home, continuing with a job and studying on a part-time local course.

Laura funded her training by saving over a number of years. Initially she considered applying for funding from the National Health Service, her employer, but decided she wanted to be independent of her organisation. It was important to Laura that she should be able to choose how and where to use the learning acquired from her training.

There are few guaranteed funding sources available. One of the most accessible is the Career Development Loan, a government deferred loan administered via some of the high street banks. Some trainees are able to make use of the limited range of other grants and loans available. There are several directories available from most reference libraries, notably *The Directory of Grant-Making Trusts*. It is worth spending some time trawling through these directories. Each trust featured will explain the application and selection procedure. In many cases they may need you to apply a year in advance. If you wish to write to trusts requesting financial support, make sure you read the eligibility criteria and ensure you fit this. *Trusts stick to their criteria ruthlessly* as they get huge numbers of requests, so don't think you can 'wing it'. You will just be wasting your time and money. It is the quality of the applications that count, not the quantity!

In one year, Rick sent out over seventy applications to grant-awarding bodies, fully aware that he didn't quite meet the eligibility criteria for many of them. The cosequence was that he received 'rejection' replies from only about twenty five and received £300 from one body for whom he was clearly eligible. The next year he sent out some twelve well-targeted applications and received modest funding from three bodies . . . time, effort and resources much better spent!

Some trainees who continue work at a job (or jobs) and study part-time, may be able to persuade employers to fund training costs. However, those employers

Appendix 1 provides you with a checklist of possible costs you may incur during training. The list, although not inclusive, [and some items may not be applicable to *your* circumstances] can be used as a general guide.

who do agree to support you may also add a clause stipulating that if you leave the organisation within a set period of time you will be liable to repay some or all of the amount they have contributed. Watch out for this!

The BAC offers a small number of bursaries [currently £500 each] to students enrolling on a BAC Accredited course. Call 01788 550 899 for details.

It is worth keeping abreast of legislation regarding such things as tax relief which change from time-to-time. Listen to budget proposals for funding education to see if you may be eligible for funding or concessions on fees. Other benefits and relief may be available at the time you read this, so it is worth consulting with the relevant authorities; DSS, Benefits Agency, Council Offices, Inland Revenue etc.

I have not had to pay for supervision because of the voluntary placement work.   *Giles*
Course costs alone, with books and travel, have been prohibitive enough.

Julia   The tax break was a welcome surprise and I was able to get a funding contribution from an organisation suggested by a trainer on the course. I see that in future years the facility to pay by instalments will not be available (without paying a surcharge) and this is a very retrograde step. I also worked in the holiday periods.

There is a chronic lack of funding for counselling training. Some people say there   *Phillipa*
are too many counsellors being trained and little overall regulation of many courses. This is very confusing for trainees and the public alike.

Gregor   I had saved up over 18 months prior to the start of my full-time Diploma, but this was still nowhere near enough. I did not do any part-time work, like working in a bar, because I felt it was better to use the spare time in 'recovery' from the days' training rather than put myself through even more grief.

I was lucky in the end. I spent what seemed liked days applying to trusts and grant-funding bodies and sent out about 50 'well-targeted' applications. I eventually got some support from a couple of bodies. I know some of my peers managed to find funding this way too but so much is based on external factors such as your background, your earlier education, where you lived, where your parents lived. I would certainly advise future students to utilise this resource and there are various directories available from the reference sections of most libraries.

My one criticism about funding was about supervision. Whilst I was supported partially by my placement clinic, all recommended individual supervisors would charge a standard rate, with no regard to student rates. When money was such a key concern, and often impacting on my counselling work, one would hope that supervisors could make a concession. The major reason is that I know I resisted one 'extra' supervision meeting at a time of an increased workload because basically it would cost me significantly more.

I often like to fantasise about winning the lottery and setting up a trust fund which   *Marion*
would help finance counsellors through their training! Perhaps if you print any of

my contribution there might be a reader who has themselves come into this sort of money! I hope this gives food for thought!!

> *Naomi*   Money problems were one of the biggest concerns for me on my course. I wish I had more in reserve than I did. I thought I had saved enough and budgeted but in the end I had to get a part-time job as a child-minder. The actual job was fine but I really didn't have the space for it when I was also trying to get myself through this very intense course.

When I sought out funding for my course, I was met with the same sort or resistance   *Pat*
I feel when I'm charging my private clients. There seems to be a feeling that counselling should be free, that people should not have to pay for something. Otherwise there is the sense that people are making money out of other peoples' misfortunes. I found that funding bodies got the impression that counselling training should also me free. Wake up and smell the overdraft!

> *Tammy*   I want to know why the vast majority of counselling books are so expensive. I find this very annoying because many trainees are working on a very limited budget. Why should we be restricted in our learning by this?

It was all the incidental aspects of training that I seemed to omit from my initial   *Hazel*
budgeting. For instance, I underestimated how much time I'd spend (or need to spend) with my peers in the pub!

• Have you budgeted for the full period of your training? (See Appendix 1.)

• Consider what 'extra' costs you pay in addition to the fees: supervision, travel (to course and placement venue), a residential weekend, other extra-curricular courses/seminars/workshops, books, tape-recording equipment and tapes, subscriptions or organisational membership, course outings and the odd weekend away from the course to recharge your batteries!

• Can you budget for a time after the end of your course when you may not find work immediately?

• Seek out directories of charitable trusts and grant-awarding bodies to see if you might qualify for application to seek funding. University careers libraries and most reference libraries will have copies.

• If you will be working part-time, is there a way your organisation can sponsor you, even if it is a token amount for books, travel etc?

• Can you get sponsorship through an organisation or professional association? Direct approaches may be most fruitful.

points to ponder

19
how person-centred was my course?

Some readers may think that the title of this chapter sounds a little strange. What does this mean, and why does this matter? It might not seem like a crucial issue to a prospective trainee, but the person-centredness of a course will have an impact on the structure, format and delivery of the training.

This counselling approach is based on a trainee developing the skills and attitudes of the 'core conditions' of congruence, empathy and unconditional positive regard. These skills and attitudes are frequently 'modelled' in the form of a 'way of being' and this is usually evident to a greater or lesser extent in the delivery of the training programme. What this means is that the tutors will adopt the core conditions as the way in which they run the course. For instance, the tutors may be congruent by speaking openly, directly and honestly to trainees rather than shying away from expressing their experience. They may also be great empathic listeners, keen to hear concerns, problems and issues trainees may be experiencing, and they may do all of this in a non-judgemental manner, i.e. offering unconditional positive regard.

The most important factor in determining the degree of person-centredness of a course, for Laura, was related to the tutors and the degree to which they were person-centred. If the tutors and the designers of the course are conducting themselves in a person-centred manner, then it is likely to be reflected in the course structure.

Another important issue in training is the proportion of responsibility given to trainees. A person-centred, or perhaps student-centred course, will offer participants significant freedom and flexibility to influence the design, content and delivery of the training. Furthermore, the management of individual learning will be the responsibility of the participants. Clearly there needs to be a core curriculum in order that there is quality, accountability and credibility. However, around this there may be opportunity for different options and choices. Since the core conditions engender self-responsibility and empowerment in a *client*, a course which offers self-responsibility and empowerment for *trainees* may make it easier for them to offer the same within the counselling room. A trainee is also likely to 'poach' styles and formats used during the training to help formulate their own way of working.

Some courses are heavily structured, unambiguous, static and inflexible. This may restrict the flow of learning for a trainee by constraining their creativity and freedom to explore. Other courses, however, offer a limited core curriculum and shift more of the responsibility for structure, content and delivery onto the trainees. The trainees would then have to wrestle with what *they* wanted, how *they* may prefer it delivered, why, when etc.

Hopefully the title for this chapter may now be starting to make more sense.

Rick was grateful for a mix of predetermined programme content and some flexibility about choosing other or new workshop topics. His course offered something like 5% of free time on the programme to allow for new topics or to spend more time on one already covered. However, there never did seem enough time for everything and he recalls frequent promises he made to himself to 'come back to that later'! Perhaps this is what much of counselling training is really about — to interest and inspire the trainee and encourage them to develop a focus of continual personal growth and personal development. Rick proposed to revisit specific topic areas after his training had ended so that he could dedicate adequate time and effort to them rather than having to skim the surface during training.

The issues raised in this chapter may be difficult to evaluate prior to starting a particular course. It should, however, be possible to speak with tutors in advance and check out the degree of flexibility and freedom that exists for trainees but the reality may still be quite different.

Yoko

For me personally, the structure of the course, particularly the Diploma year, was not heavily and purely based on Carl Rogers' work. Although I had no objections to learn and experience other theoretical approaches up to a certain point, and I was free to find and follow my personal direction theoretically and in my actual practice, I also experienced periods of conflict and concern about the loose adoption of the term person-centred and the validity of the approach in its own right.

Kenneth

I grew with others and we all grew from each other. It was safe, in our womb, as we developed. Facilitators were person-centred, they prodded but left the choosing to be personal. They were creative using time valuably, using what was presented, for growth and understanding. Yet things happened at the 'right' time. Those creations are still with me, for daily I am aware of me, of what is going on (or trying to know), assessing why I feel as I do at the happening of any single event.

Ginny

On the whole, the course was run in a student-centred way, at least as far as this was possible. The course material itself was very person-centred but it went further and also embraced Psychodynamic principles.

Tracey

I have worked with counsellors, trainers, supervisors and peers who have a similar approach to counselling, those who do not, some who are *very* Rogerian and others who make no claim to be working from a Rogerian approach. I have learned from all these people, and all of them have left some mark on my own way of working, both in what I do and what I do not do.

All the trainers on the Diploma course were very person-centred apart from one or *Dorothy*
two of the personal tutors, including mine. I also feel they had excellent modelling
from the Director. The course could have been slightly more efficiently run with
regard to its administration which tended to be done in a rather haphazard and
cavalier way.

Debbie   I feel the Diploma course was in many aspects very person-centred, especially the
self-working groups, Personal and Professional Development Groups and
Community time. The facilitators and tutors were very uninterventional and this
confused everyone for a long time because no one told us what was expected of us.

I feel this allowed my personal issues to rise naturally and taught me much about
myself but only because I had the help and challenging support of other peers
outside of these working periods. In other ways, the course developed other
counselling tools which would not normally be used in a purely person-centred
approach. The course defined itself as Heretical person-centred.

My course was very person-centred. I feel that the staff pay great attention to me *Sophie*
as a person with skills and negative points and are willing to help me on the way
to greater self-awareness without hitting me over the head with what I need to do.

Sarah   My course was run in a further education college. I feel this was eminently
unsuitable for the nature of the course. Experiential groups took place in classrooms
with upright chairs and with the noise disturbance of the rest of the college around
us. At times the material of the day left me, and others, feeling upset and in need
of 'time out'. There was nowhere suitable for this.

The course did not run in a person-centred manner. Assignment formats were
fixed, on the whole, and had to be completed in a predetermined way. Classes
followed a fairly fixed 'syllabus'. There was a very *academic* feel to the written
work. Having said this, I learned an awful lot from the presentation of the
assignments. I generally felt that I was on a predetermined conveyer belt to get me
from beginning of each stage to the end. In my experience there was little room
for the individual needs of each student throughout the course. On a positive note,
I feel my training was thorough and prepared me to work with clients in a
professional, boundaried and safe manner.

Actually, the course was not even responsible to its students. The students were *Tim*
not placed at the heart of the course, rather the heart was the institution of which
the students were placed at the lowest element. Judgement came from staff when
we refused to accept that this should be so. For instance, when we asked basic
questions about the philosophical coherence of the course, the development and
monitoring of skills work within the course, and asked why it was that the deadliest
part of the course seemed to be that of personal development.

I recall that session where two of us spent our skills session and a coffee break
(two and a half hours) trying to work out how we could challenge the fundamental
failure of the course to actually carry out the task of training in terms of philosophy,

skills and self-development. I remember the nervousness with which, very gently, very respectfully, we raised our challenge. We should have cried from the rooftops 'You're screwing us. This is what you are doing to us students, your clients'. But we did not. Counsellors are non-judgemental, they have positive regard, they are empathic. I note on our course that congruence disappeared. To be congruent in that context was to become dangerous. A threat.

Phil   Much of the way my course was run was *sensibly* person-centred. In terms of the freedom and responsibility we had, we learnt to come to terms with the ambiguity and uncertainty by being assertive and determining what we wanted. This was a frustrating, yet I feel, vital key to the development of personal power, enlightenment and self-awareness.

One almost amusing example of the absurdity of a person-centred course is as follows. We had a weekend residential where the whole 22 of us would take over a suitable venue where we would run various workshops and perhaps have the odd 'guest' speaker. It took us long enough to work, as a course, to determine which workshops would run but we spent what seemed like days in our Core Group meeting, debating an assortment of venues, dates, costs, menus, facilities, almost down to discussing the suitability of soft furnishings! This became a workshop in itself, as people like myself got incredibly frustrated about how difficult it was for us to make a group decision.

• Is the philosophy of the course you are looking at person-centred? If yes, what will this mean to you in relation to elements of the course such as assessment, feedback, self-responsibility, advice, group work and any consultation process?

points to ponder

• It may be difficult for you to answer the above question before experiencing the course. To help, you may find the following points useful:
• Identify the trainers' professional and training background.
• The course prospectus and application process will offer you a view of the course's approach.
• Discuss the course with former students, e.g. aims, objectives, styles etc.
• Meet with the course trainers prior to applying to the course to offer you further insight into the course's perspective on the approach and training.
• Identify your own approach to learning and decide if your needs and the course outline is compatible.

• Do you want a course which is purely person-centred, in terms of how it is delivered? For instance, what degree of empowerment and self-responsibility is given to trainees? Do you need quite a tight, defined and structured course, or fairly open, consultative and flexible one? Debbie,

Refer to the further reading recommended in Appendix 2 to offer you a general understanding of various therapeutic approaches. This may help you decide which approach is best suited to your own values and beliefs.

found the self-responsibility perplexing, 'The facilitators and tutors were very uninterventionist and this confused everyone for a long time because no one told us what was expected of us'.

• Would you prefer a course which is eclectic or integrative in approach, i.e. it may be based on the Person-Centred Approach but may integrate a further therapeutic approach? In Ginny's example, she points out, 'the course material itself was very person-centred but it . . . also embraced Psychodynamic principles'.

• The focus on listening, offering feedback, consulting and communicating can be a person-centred process in itself. Phil points out, though, that this can lead to difficulties. Referring to his group trying to plan a residential weekend, he volunteers, 'this became a workshop in itself, as people like myself got incredibly frustrated about how difficult it was for us to make a group decision'.

• Will you enjoy the freedom of being totally responsible for writing and the time of submitting your assignments, or find it threatening?

• You may already know the area of counselling work in which you wish to specialise (though you may not have a preference at this stage). If so, you may find it helpful to find out which counselling approaches tend to be used in your area of interest.

• Reference is made in this chapter to a 'course' operating in a person-centred manner. Is it possible that other group interactions could work in this 'person-centred' way, such as meetings at work or in team-based activities?

20
assess-
ment and
self-
appraisal

The previous chapter looked at how a course 'is' person-centred and what this might mean. This idea is expanded here by looking at the process of assessment and self-appraisal. In many respects this evaluation procedure may be person- or student-centred as well. This means an element of emphasis and responsibility may rest with the trainee to judge how they feel they are learning, developing and progressing.

Counselling training can be a lifelong road of discovery and development. We are learning and extending our awareness and insight as we accumulate experience. Part of this is the individual becoming aware of their training needs and knowing their strengths and weaknesses. This important part of being a counsellor seems to point to being our own marshals, or internal supervisors. Only we, as individuals, will know what we really need to brush up on and, of course, what we may be best at.

This concept of the *internal supervisor* or *internal evaluation* can take root early during training. Another term for this is self-appraisal. The process of this 'internal supervision' was Laura's most fundamental learning during her counselling training. During counselling sessions and in training groups she became more aware of her physical sensations and discovered that, by being open to these feelings and taking time to reflect their meaning, she was able to establish an internal dialogue which included a relationship between physical sensations, thoughts and feelings.

Many courses tap into this self-appraisal process. Each will operate slightly differently but the essence is to permit the trainee to evaluate themselves, rather than coming from the 'red pen' of the tutor which does not seem to reflect the 'personal journey' that many claim counselling training to be about.

Assessment in person-centred training includes self-assessment, peer assessment and tutor assessment. Some trainees also seek feedback from their clients and the managers of their counselling placements. There can be great value from this variety of feedback. However, what consolidates learning, is learning from the feedback is *their response* to self-assessment. This links with the process mentioned above — the *internal supervisor* or *internal evaluation*. In order to actively use or discard feedback from external sources, the trainee needs to be able to measure the value and meaningfulness of this new material in relation to their own view of the situation. In doing this, the trainee is developing a personal way of viewing the world and him/herself in it. The trainee is developing a sense of autonomy and learning to monitor and ultimately manage

The BAC Code of Ethics and Practice for Trainers (Jan 1997 — inder review) recognises the importance of having assessment methods that are in keeping with the model of therapy in clause 2.7.; 'There should be consistency between the theoretical orientation of the programme and the training methods and, where they are used, methods of assessment and evaluation (e.g. client-centred courses would normally be trainee-centred)'.

A couple of books are recommended in Appendix 2 for those readers who are worried by or have questions about assessment and assignments on counselling courses.

him/herself in a variety of situations and experiences.

To assist trainees in developing their movement towards self-assessment, person-centred counselling training generally offers a variety of forums in which to experience ways of giving, receiving and integrating feedback, e.g. supervision group, personal supervision, personal counselling, personal development group, personal journal and community meetings. Developing person-centred practice offers the opportunity of assessment from many angles, i.e. from peers, trainers, self and the client. In addition, audio and video equipment is frequently used to record the session and reflect on the process which has taken place. In developing the skills of self-assessment the trainee is also learning to trust and listen to their own responses — vital in the process of counselling. This is a process which will continue throughout your counselling career.

Rick's course required him to write several assignments, with flexibility and choice of topics. He found this flexibility actually offered him a structure in itself. In the previous chapter introduction he pointed out that due to the limit of time, he proposed to continue with his learning on certain topics later when time allowed. The final self-assessment report he wrote confirmed his belief that he felt he had fulfilled the course criteria for the Diploma and also felt personally competent and proficient enough to be worthy of this award, whilst highlighting his path for further development and training.

This self-assessment method allowed Rick the opportunity to highlight areas he needed to continue work on. An exam would probably not afford this opportunity in this candid and open way. It took Rick time to understand the self-assessment dimension to the training. It encouraged him to consider, in much greater depth, and with maturity, the insight of and feedback from his peers. Rather than feeling 'judged' by staff, he was able to confidently evaluate himself.

Rudolph

The structure of assessment was intriguing from the start. It was made fairly clear, though not explicit, what our tasks were in terms of fulfilling a course assessment criteria. We knew how many assignments we had to do and we were given initial submission dates. However, there was flexibility. If we were late in submitting an assignment, that was fine, we would simply get a delayed feedback response. I think many of us actually kept to these dates, they were the focus point. Some of my peers left the assignments until the summer but as a few found to their cost, if they 'failed' them, they had almost no time to resubmit before the Diploma cut-off date occurred.

The final part was the weirdest, simply because I had never operated in such a way. We had to complete a self-assessment report to decide whether we had met our own criteria for passing the Diploma standard. Early on, I thought, 'who on earth is going to defer themselves?' In the end about nine out of the 30 did! The focus was on us to evaluate each other and ourselves. We had responsibility to ourselves and others in the decisions we made. In the last few weeks we used our Supervision Groups to announce if we were awarding ourselves the Diploma and why. If any of our peers took issue on this, they could challenge us. It was a remarkable process and I feel probably more accurate than an examination recall test as a mark of counsellor suitability. So even the process of assessment was 'experiential'.

My only criticism about this exercise is that it was referred to by the staff as 'self-assessment' when in fact it was *partial* self-assessment. Our tutors still marked our assignments and I think I am right in saying that they could 'fail' or defer the award of our Diploma (subject to further training). What I liked about the assignment feedback from tutors was they tape-recorded their response. This was much more personal and you could really hear their comments, rather than just reading them.

Diana

The essay marking was always done by two tutors, i.e. one's personal tutor and the course director. There has been more self-assessment on the MSc than on the Diploma and, having now become used to that concept, I feel it is of great value in giving me the ability to monitor myself more closely and honestly.

But in terms of essays, they were indeed a struggle. Because I had done nursing and had not gone to university this was my first experience of what I would term a truly academic piece of work and I found it frightening, challenging and difficult.

Sally

The assignments are given feedback on cassette which is very effective and communicates more than a written note or mark would do. I have to admit that I would also have liked a mark — but I know this is my teaching background coming out.

Gordon

I recognise that the greatest change in my work came when an assessment was given not in terms of passes and failures but in terms of challenge and trust that I could go further and that the tutor would hold me whilst I did that. And what I did was to find a dangerous, unconventional, challenging-to-academe voice which needed a political support, as well as checking and supporting whilst I found an emotional and intellectual veracity and validity.

Cynthia

Scanning the course of my training experience that year, I believe that assessing my own development and competence and receiving honest feedback were both essential parts of my learning. Progressively during the first few months I found myself well under pressure striving to meet my personal high expectations. On the one hand, I was able to build up a case-load at a manageable-to-me pace (up to three clients until Christmas) in order to offer a safe service to my clients and maximise my own learning. On the other hand, I had thrown myself into intensive skills practice (video-making) at college and hard work at home (reading, processing training input and experiences, reflecting, client notes etc.).

Sarah

We didn't have any formal essays or assignments. The assessment of our work was part self-assessment and part peer-assessment of our work. Additionally there was supervision of all our counselling work and training sessions. This included supervision assessment in the form of feedback of our practice and the thinking behind it.

Self-assessment was difficult to begin with. It was difficult to know how you were doing in comparison to others. Now I appreciate what this was all about. It makes me think more about what I am doing. It has given me the responsibility for my own training. It also encourages me to seek help when I need it.

points to ponder

- To what extent is your forthcoming course self-assessed? Do you understand what this demands of you, and if so, are you happy with this? Cynthia found this most enlightening, 'I believe that assessing my own development and competence and receiving honest feedback were both essential parts of my learning'.

- Do you need any support or help with writing essays? Many of us have not written essays for many years so this can be quite a challenging task.

- Are you clear what is expected of you during the course in terms of assignments and assessment? For instance, assignments, supervision groups, individual supervision, peer group work, skills practice, placement work, residential course work, lectures, seminars, workshops and any other tasks?

- What mode of feedback will you get from staff, peers and placement managers? For example, staff may give feedback on your assignments via one-to-one consultations, paper responses or, as Sally experienced, 'on cassette' which she found, 'very effective and communicates more than a written note or mark would'. Gordon highlights the difference in quality of feedback, 'I recognise that the greatest change in my work came when an assessment was given not in terms of passes and failures but in terms of challenge and trust'. Peers may give feedback individually or within the confines of predetermined groups, such as supervision group or personal development groups. Placement managers may have their own manner for communicating feedback, by letter or meeting.

- Should you need to repeat some aspect of the training to meet the course criteria, are you aware of your responsibilities and what is expected of you?

- Are you aware of who (and how) to contact should you wish to make a complaint or lodge an appeal for any assessed work?

21
reaching
the end of
the course

The end of a counselling course can provoke as much anxiety as the beginning. During counselling training, groups of people from all walks of life will have meshed together, sometimes sparring with, sometimes helping each other. The sheer intensity of the course, and within this, the caring and sharing experienced, may have helped develop a deep bond between individuals and with the group as a whole. Very few training experiences will challenge you as much as counselling training. We hope the preceding chapters will have given you flavours of this.

During training, we are encouraged to drop our guards, confront our defences and open ourselves up to scrutiny and self-exploration. No amount of safety and support will prevent us feeling intensely vulnerable and raw at times. That is not to say that you will be thrown into a lion's den to confront your inner demons, but just to remind you of the potential depths that may be plumbed during counsellor training.

The case-studies featured here illustrate the range of feelings attached to the ending of a course. Several draw a parallel between the training experience and a one-to-one personal relationship. There is often a real sense of loss when a course ends.

Laura felt bereft at the end of her training. She was not only finishing her course but also leaving her home-town, her home, family, friends and dogs. Once Laura had moved, she realised just how deep the level of community was that she had experienced on the course. It was a difficult process for her to move on, but the positive experience of real community stayed with her. It has helped her understand what is positive for *her* way of living.

At the end of his course, Rick was aware of a feeling of real loss but found it difficult to clearly identify. He knew he would keep up with most of the friends made so he would not be losing out there. He had lined up further training so he would not lose ongoing development and he was retaining contact with the course staff as a result of the further training. His conclusion was that the feeling of loss was due to an accumulation of things including the familiarity, personal closeness and expectations of the frequent individual and group challenges, the sense of excitement felt during nervous exchanges and the apprehensions felt when he risked being real, open and honest.

During the last month of his Diploma course, Rick felt an indistinguishable mix of dread, hopeful expectation, relief, loss for potentially losing contact with some people, and hope that he *would* lose contact with other people!

I feel very privileged to have had the opportunity to train in this way on such excellent person-centred courses — and with such interesting and experienced people who have modelled the person-centred ethos so well — well, most of them have! I do value the experiences I have had and how it has facilitated my learning and process. Especially when I hear of others who have been on courses not run from a person-centred base and whose experiences have been less than satisfactory, leaving them not feeling affirmed and in some cases even feeling abused.

Sam

Tim

Completing my course, I feel that what I have been living through is a reiteration of being abused. Instead of working through a coherent course founded in philosophy (of research and counselling), of skills (of finding an appropriate way of living and working the research), or knowing myself in the process, I have been reduced to being an object of compassion — all disempowered, of losing speech. That even writing this becomes a way of resistance to being dumbed.

Coming up to the end of my training I am still grappling with the questions. The politics of oppression have been named and put into little boxes — have they then been *done*? Fortunately I know both people who feel positive about 'counselling' and those who are wonderfully sceptical. This creates more questions than answers and is a constant source of learning for me.

Kitty

With them I explore the personal, the political and the spiritual, questions of oppression, fundamental questions about the individual versus environment and questions about whether counselling can make a difference. As well as having a beer or two I hasten to add! With peers and alone I think about my own person-centredness — what was Carl Rogers saying? What am I doing? What do I think and feel about what Rogers said?

Person-centred training was the right approach for me and I certainly have no regrets, only questions. I would imagine that Rogers would be more than happy with this!

Fi

By the end of the course I felt that I had truly grown as a person. I was more aware of processes going on between individuals, between others and myself and within myself. I gained in confidence and became aware when I was being judgemental and tried to overcome this. I feel I became more tolerant, also more ambitious and keen to do counselling at a higher level and have now applied to a marriage counselling agency to be trained as a couple's counsellor.

I remember the end of my training with an over riding feeling. Relief! I was knackered physically, emotionally, psychologically and mentally. I had been to hell and back. But I had also been to heaven and back. I had become a bigger person, maybe a person at last and at least. I did not want to do any counselling for several months after the end. I wanted a break. Ironically, after my Diploma I continued on with studies in the shape of a Masters degree. But it was odd. Despite having the link of going back to the same campus I was feeling a real sense of loss. I felt I could never capture or experience a year like that ever again. I had felt I had climbed my way up Everest but that having got to the top and arrived safely back

Jerry

down that no challenge could beat that. I would have to find my challenges from more frequent smaller peaks!

Anne-Marie   The end of the course for me introduced me to the whole idea of 'endings' and how we move on from things, or not, as the case may be. I'm not quite sure what it is but I'm now more aware of other transitions and endings in my life and they all generate a greater meaning now. Perhaps this brings back the ending of my counselling course. In some ways this was longed for but I also miss part of it.

The best thing that happened on the course was the ending and getting back into the real world again. Hurrah!   *Helena*

points to ponder

- How much importance or consideration does your course put on the ending of the training (and on the end of each term)? As trainee counsellors, we will learn the importance of managing the 'end' of a counselling relationship. Sometimes, the same may apply for us reaching an ending stage in our development.

- What support can you call upon, outside the course, to help you finish training and move on to *your* next stage?

- What support can you get from peers and staff to help you through the transition of ending the training course?

- Which members of staff can give you advice on what to do *after* finishing your course, e.g. further academic study, or seeking work in a particular work context?

- The end of a course can mark a change in your life. Like any transition this can be welcomed or dreaded. As Jerry points out, he seems to have felt 'a real sense of loss'.

- There seem to be those who dread the end of the course and those who welcome it, such as Helena who felt the ending was the 'best thing that happened on the course'!

- Another point that Jerry raises is the exhaustion that he felt at the end, 'I was knackered, physically, emotionally, psychologically and mentally. I had been to hell and back. But I had also been to heaven and back'. It doesn't sound like we could get a better description of the ups and downs than this!

- Could you give yourself a treat for having made it through the course?!

22
how to improve the training experi- ence

This chapter may be of particular interest to trainers, tutors and course staff. The case-studies demonstrate a range of issues which were important to former trainees. Many courses will have evaluation questionnaires at stages throughout, and at the end of, the course where suggestions for improvement can be made. It is encouraging that some institutions actively seek ways to improve the structure, content and delivery of training and it is they who are 'person-centred'. This will facilitate improvement in the quality of course delivery and subsequent integrity of the training of person-centred counselling.

Those who contributed to this book were given the opportunity to suggest how their training experiences might have been improved. Some took this as an opportunity to vent their frustrations and anger about what they endured. The reader will note the length of the case-studies given and this seems to suggest that several contributors really want to make constructive comments.

This chapter was not intended to be an assault on courses or of counselling *per se* but it has been retained to reflect the really useful points which are raised. No one wrote specifically about positive experiences they wanted to reinforce, rather, they wished to comment on frustrations or 'negative' experiences and offer advice for change. It might have been better balanced to hear from positive experiences but on reflection we thought that this is covered, indirectly, in many other chapters in this book.

Rick would like to have had more time allocated to working with counselling dilemmas, perhaps through workshops or acting out a range of scenarios typical for different counselling contexts. He remembers attending an interview for a counselling position. One of the tasks was for the group of interviewees to discuss the dilemmas indicated by several specified client/counsellor conflict scenarios. He was acutely aware that he hadn't a clue how to start prioritising actions. He claimed that every situation should be evaluated on their individual merits and that there was never any cut-and-thrust answer — he thought that this was a cop-out.

Laura would have liked a longer period of training. It went incredibly quickly for her and she felt she would have benefited from further time to reflect on her development and practice. Most counsellors find a way of doing this. One of Laura's ways was to contribute to the development of this book. Ultimately, Laura feels most trainees would benefit if some form of reflection period is built into the course training experience — by having quarterly update meetings where trainees could feed back and share their subsequent 'post-training' reflection.

The course structure was less than ideal. There were three stages to the course, however, successful completion of one part of the course did not necessarily mean one would have the opportunity to progress onto the next stage. There was a selection at each stage. I am not against the notion that the course tutors may feel some people are not suitable to progress to the next level, however, it became clear very early on that the selection was very much linked to a 'numbers game'. To ensure that the later stages of the course were full, there were many more people on the earlier stages than there were places on the later stage.

Sophie

This had the effect of placing a great deal of stress and pressure on everyone on the course. I know that I found this a very difficult aspect of the course. I feel it had the effect of putting enormous pressure on me to get the highest marks possible for the written assignments. I feel that it left little space for the personal development, growth and contemplation that is so key to such a course.

I feel that greater emphasis should have been given to what impact the course would have on trainees' time. I am not against part-time courses. I think that a period of a few years to grow and develop is a good thing. I guess what I feel should have been made clear at the start is that, once in the later stages of the course, around three days equivalent per week of time would be required to undertake and complete the various course demands and that on top of this, study time needs to be added.

Sandy

I am aware of one concern I have but I wish to talk about it as a developmental opportunity rather than a problem issue. Trainees will, by the nature of their attendance, be testing out a range of interpersonal dynamics which will come into play. We may like some people and not others and all that is fine. But there doesn't seem to be much in the way of a focus from trainers to attend to dynamics which they may contribute to. In some ways I'm thinking of abuses of power and status. Not only might there be a parent/child interaction but there may also be control and even sexually suggestive issues. I'm reminded of a male trainer who seemed to treat several female students in a very condescending way. On the other hand, a female trainer seemed to persistently applaud the comments of one particular male student. I don't feel he was *that* right all the time. I'm sure the trainer had a thing about him. But all this affected the dynamics. We just need to be more aware of how we are all interacting, but specifically to include trainers into this.

Perhaps my solution would be to have some form of 'team development days' in a way that various group exercises operate to cleanse the community of any hidden agendas. I don't know how this would work but it does seem to be important that trainers can be expected to open themselves, their thoughts, feelings and desires (if it impinges on the course).

There are many issues connected with this whole episode of counselling training. As a trainer myself, who works in a person-centred way, I would never fail a student without first giving them the opportunity to put things right. The training is where the person-centredness and good example should begin. I believed the

Tony

trainer to be my friend and felt betrayed by his behaviour — she must have had a boundary problem for me to feel this way or was it my expectations were too great?

It has made me look at this whole issue of training. So, I have to write good essays that meet someone's criteria in order to qualify to become a 'bona fide' counsellor? I don't think so. I have met people with Diplomas who just have no people skills. I hear stories from students who have had counselling experiences which would make your hair curl. I have met trainers and counsellors who are on the 'I am' bandwagon. This is not for me. I do not mean to sound angry. I have become disappointed and disillusioned by the whole profession and the way early training is delivered. How will a Diploma make me any better at my job than I am now? My experience has made me very nervous.

With regard to person-centred courses, they should be run in a person-centred way. The focus should be on the individual not the establishment in which they are run. I believe every counsellor should be trained initially in the person-centred way and this should be the foundation on which to build an integrated approach. My own experience of person-centred counselling training was disappointing and left me with feelings of little worth and much insecurity. Had it not been for the support of my supervisor, the counselling profession would have lost a personality with the ability to help others heal themselves in positive ways. That would have been a great shame. This has not deterred me from continuing in my work but it has made me question how training is delivered and by whom . . . and I question myself here too.

Jenny   The thing that concerns me most is the lack of insurance. I was the only person in my group of 20 students who holds professional indemnity and that is given through the British Psychological Society to cover any work that I do as a Psychologist. Given the nature of the work and the material we are dealing with, there seems to be no protection against litigation either for students on the course, clients of students or indeed clients of qualified counsellors.

Although there have not been many cases to date, there have been one or two reported in 'Counselling' Journal. We are becoming, as a society, more willing to make people accountable if they have been unprofessional or negligent, therefore, it would seem prudent that this should be addressed. Other professions (nurses, midwives, social workers, doctors, lawyers etc.) insist on this kind of cover to protect the profession, the professional and the client. I am concerned that counselling courses do not insist on this.

The other aspect of counselling training that concerns me is the apparent lack of support for some students who are obviously struggling emotionally. The training ethos seems to be to teach the student to learn to recognise their own needs and seek out help and support either from their peers or from the tutors. However, I think that some people are not able to do this for whatever reason and do really struggle.

I do appreciate the rationale behind this but find the *sink or swim* approach hard to take. The idea seems to be that those who can't cope will simply leave, a sort of process of natural selection? I am still trying to work out if this is my *need* to help or support or a genuine recognition of poor practice in terms of student training.

One small piece of advice for courses. There are certain decisions that perhaps should be made by tutors/course directors. My peers seemed unable to make a decision about anything and, yes, I was as guilty as everyone else. For instance, everyone wanted to be so aware of everybody else's views they (yes, and me too) failed to assert themselves effectively.

Phil

In replying to this chapter prompt, I would like to offer several concerns rather than advice. I can appreciate the detailed planning that goes into the development and implementation of counselling training but, having said that, it is imperative that such training is a developmental process in itself. It should never become a static process otherwise it defeats the object. So I like a degree of personal and collective group responsibility that is placed on us.

But I would like to see a definition of this at the beginning of training. Collective group responsibility is probably a new concept for most of us. We need to be able to understand this in order for us to work with it. Perhaps it might be useful to have a workshop or seminar just on this topic. This will also tap into many personal issues, such as assertiveness and confidence, a vital element of personal development and awareness. OK, so this *concern* has evolved into *advice*!

A real concern I have is the credibility issue. I now have a Diploma and somehow believe I am probably a better counsellor than those who don't. Now I probably *do* have better skills but the whole message, that I have this ominous Diploma and am thus a professional, doesn't feel right. I feel I am a disciple of this award, encouraging counsellors without this qualification to strive towards this. Maybe this is the right thing to do?

I have thought of another point. There are a large number of counselling courses now and this seems to be a growth industry. The downside is the lack of jobs. The demand for counsellors does not meet the accelerating supply of budding and enthusiastic practitioners. The real downside is the demotivation that occurs after training when people intent on working as full-time counsellors find there are really no opportunities. All courses have a responsibility to explain this to students, both at the application and selection stage, as well as towards the end of training — to ease the transition onto civvy street.

Chris

I realise that my concern may be restricted to the trainers on my particular course and so may not be representative but I was always aware of a sort of aloofness which pervaded from the trainers. They may not have meant to have this effect but it certainly came through. Many of my fellow course workers felt the same. It may have been something about their experience and qualifications but there was always a 'them and us' feeling.

There was a consensus towards the end of the course that after Christmas, with *Pete*
academic deadlines to meet, people tacitly withdrew their energies from the
experiential learning opportunities. There was still the peer-group assessment of
papers, the close work in tutorial groups which worked better for some. However,
for others it was seriously affected by people withdrawing from close interaction
as they focused on meeting the academic criteria.

I believe that since then, there has been an acknowledgement that too much was
expected with the twin goals of person-centred process and academic rigour. The
exam requirement has been dropped, so limiting the external expectations and
pressure to regurgitate theory. In retrospect, the part-timers who were taking the
course over two years had time to reflect on their experiences and possibly build
this into their work, whereas for the full-timers it was more intense. The learning
outcomes are naturally individualised but it would have been interesting to have
followed up the perceptions between the two groups.

points to
ponder

- The case-studies here sought to offer advice on how the training experience
  could be improved, based on a retrospective evaluation by former trainees.
  Sophie, for instance, felt her course structure 'less was ideal', proposing
  that, 'greater emphasis should have been given to what impact the course
  would have on trainees' time'.

- Prior to training, consider how you would react if you are not happy with
  something. Do you let others take the plunge, do you act reasonably or do
  you over react? What and where is the balance?

- It is good to hear from Tony, 'As a trainer myself . . . I would never fail a
  student without first giving them opportunity to put things right'. This sounds
  like the real way in which people learn. Lessons learned from mistakes can
  be, in some cases, much more memorable, long-lasting and impactful than
  lessons from successes.

- As in any environment made up of several groups of people, there can be a
  tendency to collude with problems and fall into the 'politics' of a situation.
  Consider how you might work with this in a constructive manner.

- The skill of giving and receiving constructive feedback is not easy. Much of
  counselling training relies on communicating views and relating with a
  diverse group of individuals. The experience of making suggestions or
  offering advice can be invaluable to yourself and to those who you want to
  offer the advice to.

- Jenny covers an interesting point. In her third paragraph, she voices her concern about the 'lack of support for some students who are obviously struggling emotionally'. While she acknowledges the emphasis on self-responsibility, she recognises 'that some people are not able to do this for whatever reason and do really struggle'.

• You will probably have many different experiences throughout your training. You may find it helpful to think about how you can pass on your valuable experience to others such as trainers, peers and future trainees. You may discover that you can assimilate your thoughts and feelings during the experience and offer it to others through feedback. It may be that insight into an experience is retrospective and you will need to think about what to do about this knowledge, if anything. In many ways this book is a result of our wish to acknowledge and share our experiences.

23
the experi-
ence
of being
person-
centred

Chapter 19 looked at the person-centredness of *the course*. This chapter takes a step to the side and explores the *individual* or *trainee experience* of being person-centred, or struggling to be person-centred.

Clearly, person-centred values are also the ones polished as skills by the counsellor for the therapeutic hour but it seems that many trainees want to develop these attitudes as part of *their* 'way of being', i.e. their way of living life as a whole. Such efforts could be regarded as an integral part of personal development. People seem to vary in their views as to whether *being* person-centred *in life* is necessary to *being* a person-centred *counsellor.* On the one hand, we might like to think that how we are outside of the therapeutic hour is consistent with how we are within it. On the other hand, some counsellors talk of getting 'into counselling mode' prior to seeing clients. This refers to the preparation process they go through, and they would argue that the importance is in *being* person-centred as a counsellor, and that it is somewhat irrelevant how a person is otherwise. Both trainees and experienced practitioners alike, wrestle with the two sides of this debate.

Rick feels it is impossible for him as a person to fully adhere to the core conditions out of the counselling room. Certainly, he can adopt the principles and similar attitudes to valuing and respecting people, but complete obedience (as though it were a set of rules) seems impractical. His point is that there are times when he doesn't want to be empathic. (For instance, he is unlikely to feel the sorrow and dismay felt by the French when they lose a rugby international against Scotland!) However, he finds he is generally more congruent, perhaps tactfully and sensitively congruent — he will express his emotions more and have a greater openness about how he relates to people. Furthermore, his enhanced valuing of people leads him to being less judgemental than he once was. So in this sense, Rick is living more of the core conditions: his way of being, the way he lives his life does tie in more closely with these conditions.

In both day-to-day life, and in the counselling environment, Laura can struggle with valuing every human being despite their behaviour. At times, she finds it difficult to divorce the individual from their actions and see the person behind. An individual's behaviour can sometimes be so dazzling or repulsive that it can be a struggle to maintain one's sense of unconditional positive regard.

The following case-studies will illuminate what being person-centred means to several former trainees. It is probably worth mentioning that this insight can take some time to achieve and so is unlikely to be fully understood until you have some experience on your course and in practice with clients. However, the concept of 'being person-centred' does come up during training and it was felt this chapter would offer an insight into this position.

I think I had always been a warm, open, respectful and caring person, yet I had never really been aware of this. I know that it is not possible to live a double life. To be person-centred is a way of life or as Rogers said, 'a way of being'.

Gareth

This is the way I now live, in the hope that I might, in my behaviour, influence those with whom I come into contact so they, too, can be more open and human to others. So often I believe that it is possible to be connected to other human beings if each is open to this connection, as if in a spiritual or mystical way.

I heard the statement, 'be person-centred always'. For me that was the key to my overall learning. It was not for five hours a week or in a session but needed to be always. How was I to transform 42 years of life into understanding of a different way of being by trying to live this on a part-time basis? I needed to 'live' it.

My person-centredness has been challenged and I am OK with that. I find myself in a solid place from that which has grown within me. I am glad I had no prescriptive mechanisms to carry me along. Self-understanding in its simplest yet most complex form, no jargon, facets presented then used as tools for life, my life and that of others. To be present with others while in a struggle, for them to have company while they discover themselves.

Professional development is ongoing and important to me. I will work towards accreditation. Whether my next step is to become a Supervisor or to take a Masters, I don't know yet. I am open to the experience.

Carol I feel that the person-centred values that were already present within me, became, as a result of being on the Diploma, much more of an integrated part of me. Since beginning my full-time counselling job, my confidence took another step forward as I began to connect person-centred values with theory in a much more detailed way. I became aware of how many parts of myself were gradually integrating both within myself and my work. I felt that person-centredness was so much part of me that I often found it difficult to separate the elements of it out for the purpose of study.

Throughout the year I enjoyed the exploratory excitement of sharing ideas and value differences within the small discussion group which I was part of. Soon enough I realised that my almost provocative enthusiasm for the Person-Centred Approach ran the risk of offending a number of people who didn't seem to share my heartfelt views, although this wasn't my intention.

Joan

It was particularly challenging and useful for me to immerse myself into rigid theories and ideological conflicts which I was unwilling to ignore. Driven by the revolutionary spirit of respect for my subjective reality, I was motivated to adopt an open but critical stance towards any rigidity of thoughts and practice.

Rebecca   I feel that my style of counselling is not 'purist' *and* I feel certain that my style is person-centred. I read very early in my training a book with the title 'If you meet the Buddha on the road, kill him'. Apart from wondering why the Buddha is assumed to be a man, and apart from my difficulty with the allusion to killing someone, I feel it is wonderfully appropriate to share.

    Rogers has become a guru, and while I feel warmed and inspired by much of what he wrote, I also feel that he was, no more or less than any of us, a person of his time. My own experience includes a very real sense that naming and showing some understanding of the effects of outside pressures in the counselling room can have a liberating effect and gives empathy a much more solid and real quality. This recognises that a person doesn't come to you in isolation and that you have some understanding of how the world impacts on their life.

Working as a therapist with children, young people and adults, I have, I hope, *Tabi* found a place where I fit in, at least for the moment. My work with children is very much focused around a Cognitive/Behavioural approach which by its very nature is directive but within this programme there are plenty of opportunities to move into a more child-centred way of working. This is particularly so in the early stages of work with a child when play is used to explore issues. I have found child-centred play therapy to be very effective with children who are unwilling or unable to speak.

In the counselling work that I do with young people and adults I use a person-centred approach into which I incorporate a number of different therapeutic models as the clients' needs change and develop throughout the counselling process. My use of the Person-Centred Approach reflects my own firmly held belief that people have within themselves the ability to do or be anything they want, if only someone has the courage to believe in them and let them believe in themselves.

For me this is what counselling is all about — empowering others. It has been a constant issue for me throughout training and I am shocked by how little is actually written about this in the counselling relationship. This is something I consider to be a fundamental goal of the counselling process. I hope Rogers *et al* would agree with me. But empowerment is also one of the hardest things to do well. My favourite analogy is of letting go of the back of a child's bike when they first learn to ride. You know that if you don't let go they will never learn to ride, yet if you do, they run the risk of getting hurt.

I spend my time with my clients supporting them, sometimes just staying close to them, close enough to catch them if they start to wobble. And then comes the time when I have to let go and hope that they can stay upright. After all, getting back on that bike after a painful tumble can be even harder than getting on in the first place. The reward is the independence and freedom it brings when you have learned to ride.

Counselling is ultimately the most rewarding and powerful of experiences. With each of my clients it has been the greatest privilege to be invited to share in a small part of their journey and to watch them walk on without me into a terrifying world, full of confidence and hope. To conclude, the Person-Centred Approach, for me, is about enabling others to use their own unique gifts and insights to become more fully human, to be the person God meant them to be. And while it is very hard to do, not only to let go of our own insecurities and fears but also to deal with the fears of our clients, we begin this journey of discovery.

Curt   The core conditions of empathy, congruence and unconditional positive regard, when applied to a therapeutic process open up to me a *brave new world*. It is not like a masonic code or a secret handshake but it is a very real and alive process. And it works too. It took me quite some time during training, despite many sceptical challenges, to trust in this approach but my faith, my training and above all my work with my clients has shown to me that it can work.

I would be both arrogant and unrealistic to claim that it always works. It doesn't always and part of my professionalism is recognising my own limitations and that of the approach.

In writing about 'being person-centred', I would say that this has certainly impacted on my values and beliefs. But I would quite categorically state that I do not live my full life in a person-centred way. I may aspire to this but I am human. Sometimes I am judgemental, sometimes I say a white lie, sometimes I hide my true feelings, but for me that is fine. I am aware of when I do this and so this is what rationalises this acceptance. I have the choice over who I am, what I do and how I do it.

I know when I piss people off, when I hurt them, when I annoy them. It is this sensitivity and awareness which is what I believe to be the person-centred way of living.

But what was it like doing person-centred training? Liberating. When I learned about the core, necessary and sufficient conditions for therapeutic change to occur I learned that being person-centred also applied to me, not only to my focus on my client. It worked for me too. In order to get my needs met, I needed to be 'me-focused'. I needed to apply the three most significant conditions to myself — to be congruent with myself, to be empathic with myself and to be unconditionally self-accepting and respecting.   *Steph*

I learned about my own internalised conditions of worth. I felt a huge sense of relief that I could *listen* to my guts and get the message I'd wanted to hear for decades! Along with my growing awareness of my true feelings I also started to be responsible for my own feelings. I gradually learned not to project them onto others, not assuming that someone was thinking/feeling the way I imagined. I felt both frightened and exhilarated as I learned to take responsibility for getting my own needs met within a group.

The more I write this, the more I keep asking myself 'But what *was* it like being in person-centred counselling training?' My training was experiential, therefore, how else could I describe it without describing the process or journey. However, I believe, and I hear from colleagues, that my training process and experiences mirrors theirs.

Because my training was experiential I developed an understanding of how my clients feel during their process. I developed an understanding of what it feels like to be stuck, embarrassed as a client, ashamed to be in front of a therapist. I learned from personal experience how important it was/is for me to *feel* unconditionally accepted at whatever stage. I experienced the sometimes frail joy of being fully and actively listened to. I heard my peers reflect what I had said in a way that confirmed for me that they fully heard and respected me.

points to ponder

- What does being 'person-centred' mean to you now, at this stage in planning your training?

- Are there any times as a counsellor when offering the core conditions of empathy, congruence and unconditional positive regard would, for you, be inappropriate? If so. why? Are there any exceptions to the rule?

- If you believe you offer the core conditions *only* in a therapeutic relationship, what impact does *not* offering such conditions in your day-to-day life have on your counsellor/client relationship?

- Perhaps you know someone who seems to be very much in touch with living their lives in a person-centred way (maybe with no knowledge of counselling) — what impact does this person have on you?

- Some people may 'feel' person-centred and others not. Carol, for instance, explains that the 'person-centred values that were already present within [her] became . . . much more of an integrated part of [her]'. However, Curt sees himself slightly differently, 'I would quite categorically state that I do not live my full life in a person-centred way. Sure, I aspire to this but I am human.'

section f

the future

Perhaps we embark on training with a purpose, as a means to an end. Some of us will aim to learn to use counselling skills. In this case, such skills would be integrated into a way of working to complement and supplement the current job roles and tasks. For others there will be a goal to become a counsellor in any of a wide range of contexts. And some will see it as a step towards personal development, regardless of career and professional outcome.

One thing is clear, finding work as a counsellor is not easy. There has been a surge of acceptability, understanding and support for the profession. Yet even with this enthusiastic endorsement there are still not the level of paid positions to meet the community need for counselling. However, there seems to be a huge demand for voluntary sector free counselling. The problem here is a financial one. For instance, in Primary Care, there are some NHS Trusts who will employ counsellors as a practice resource. Other NHS Trusts will not employ counsellors but will make referrals to voluntary and community-based counselling agencies. This will influence the degree of demand for counselling opportunities in the respective NHS Trust area.

Few counsellors are in a position to be able to offer their services free, although there is some support for the view that counselling should be free for clients at the source. This means service provision is paid for by someone else. Some large organisations will possibly employ a dedicated company counsellor or they may buy in a counselling 'package', i.e. an Employee Assistance Programme delivered by a network of independent counsellors. This resource will then be available to employees of this organisation. For people not connected to, or working in, such organisations there are voluntary or private sector agencies. Some will be free of charge, some will opt for a sliding scale for fees and some ask for voluntary contributions. The more free services become available, the more competition private practitioners will face.

The only way to be prepared for the future is to become part of it. Several counselling associations and affiliate bodies produce their own newsletters, brochures or journals and these seek to inspire and update members with topical and contemporary issues. Conferences, workshops and meetings can also help to provide a forum for debate, creative development and insight. Being part of this wave ensures that you have the chance to go with the flow rather than being swept away.

Chapter 24 will give you a flavour of what some former trainees are doing now, how they got there and perhaps where they aim to go next. This may help

You will learn that person- or client-centred therapy is effective in a wide range of settings, though you may have to argue your case as there is a little prejudice against person-centred ways of working in some sectors. There are many person-centred counsellors working in primary health care, psychiatric day-care and educational settings. Voluntary agencies offering free counselling services include: Victim Support, Rape Crisis and many community-based projects aimed at, for example, young people, such as 'Off The Record'.

Both BAPCA and BAC are good organisations to join for networking and learning about job opportunities (and the BAC journal carries job adverts). Contact information in Appendix 3.

you consider potential employment options prior to starting training.

Chapter 25 represents a sort of 'any other business' section, encouraging those who have contributed to this book to volunteer a response to the question, 'If there was one thing you wish you'd known before you had started training ,what would it be?' The responses are as varied as they are useful. The comments may help you reflect on some unanswered questions you may have. This final chapter will feature some themes or comments which might have been brought up earlier under different chapters. But the objective of Chapter 25 is to seek out what people *wished they had known* and to present a checklist to help you choose your route into and through counselling training.

Of course, we end with the rationale for the very start. The one thing which most former trainees wanted prior to starting training was a book which reviewed the experience of counselling training! It is hoped that this has been thought-provoking, insightful, and above all, enjoyable.

person-centred
counselling
training

24
where are
you now?

As we set about compiling this chapter, we realised that perhaps it may be a useful chapter with which to start reading this book! It reveals what former trainees are doing now — this may inspire you with hope or fill you with dread. As with any academic or vocational training, people have a good idea of what they want to do once training is completed. Those of us who may have taken a first university degree may be familiar with the feeling towards the end — the belief that the world is our oyster. As some readers will know, the reality of higher education in the twenty-first century is that a degree, for instance, is not a sure passport into a particular profession or career. The same probably applies to professional counselling qualifications.

The truth is that there are many more trained counsellors graduating from courses than there are jobs. However, this should not deter people who wish to seek out such positions. What often happens is that even those who start training with a strong desire to become counsellors, will learn through the experience of the training itself that they do not want to be employed as a professional counsellor. Although some will drop out of training along the way, others will finish the course, still knowing that they have no intention of pursuing a career in counselling.

The motivation and reason for embarking on counselling training will be the key factor in determining how you progress and develop your career. Some people train to learn counselling skills as a valuable add-on specialism to their current job. For instance, many who study on a part-time course will do so whilst retaining a job, which might include any role within the 'caring' professions or beyond. For them, the end of training will mark a time when they return more fully to their day jobs. However, even those who are training whilst still employed may opt for a change in career once training is completed. Their values, skills and aspirations may well encourage them to seek new opportunities.

On a more positive note, there is a great range of counselling employment contexts available. Who knows what your preferences or chosen specialism might be if and when you complete your training. There are paid and non-paid opportunities to practice counselling post-graduation — and you will read below that there are many reasons why someone may choose unpaid work.

On the paid front, this can further split down into either self-employed or salaried positions. Being self-employed usually means a counsellor sees clients privately. Options for private work may range from renting a suitable room, anywhere from £2–£20 per hour, from an established counselling centre or

Work with an EAP tends to be freelance where you may be called on demand to see clients at their place of work or at a location away from the workplace. EAPs tend to offer a range of employee services including financial advice, specific issue support (substance use, domestic violence), outplacement support (a sanitised term for redundancy), other advice and information services and counselling. In fact, counselling tends to represent probably only about 20% of the work of an EAP.

BAC has special-interest groups for members working in various settings, such as counselling in the workplace, in medical settings, in education and so on. More information about the types of settings in which counselling is practiced can be obtained from BAC. Contact details in Appendix 3.

from serviced business premises. Some counsellors have a 'day job' to which they add some private client work during the evenings or at weekends.

Other salaried positions may include:
• counselling in Primary Health Care (in a G.P. practice),
• counselling in statutory mental health settings (e.g. as a mental health support worker, or as a counsellor in a mental health team),
• counselling in mental health organisations (e.g. MIND),
• counselling in specialist mental health units (e.g. for substance use),
• counselling in specialist health areas (e.g. HIV/AIDS, well-woman clinics),
• counselling as a supplement to social services (e.g. after adoption),
• counselling in a college or university,
• counselling in custodial settings, (e.g. in prisons or special units),
• counselling in the work environment (e.g. in occupational health departments),
• counselling for an Employee Assistance Programme (EAP) provider.

In the health sector there is a range of services using volunteers and paid counsellors. There will be services catering for people with, or relatives of those afflicted by, a range of conditions, such as depression, alcoholism, drug dependency, ME, MS, cancer etc. Others cater for people in specific situations such as homelessness, rehabilitation centres, victims of abuse etc. There are 'self-help' or support groups which are run for and by people with experience of specific mental and physical illnesses and here, too, there may be opportunities for counselling work. Find out what is available in your area in order to get a good picture of the kinds of opportunities available.

Some people prefer to work as unpaid volunteers. They may, on completion of their training, decide to continue in their current employment and simply dedicate their counselling work to the voluntary sector. Others will use volunteer work to gain experience and counselling hours in order to gain accredited status with a professional body such as BAC. Then, when they are accredited, they will apply for jobs in counselling.

Rick's counselling work experience has included a wide range of contexts. However, rather than making a deliberate decision to explore the various facets of different contexts, he was motivated by the need to do any kind of work so that he could support himself during his next stage of training — a research degree. It was also essential to continue with client work, to 'keep his hand in'. During this period of work, he discovered the many diverse contexts and environments in which person-centred counselling can effectively operate. This has encouraged him to explore and study aspects of management styles and practices which may be able to draw from such philosophy.

Laura's current work focuses on person-centred *learning* rather than *counselling*. However, she finds the principles are the same. She is able to combine working with the individual as well as the group process. By using a person-centred approach, Laura can work with students to identify their own way of learning and ultimately their own path.

After my Diploma I wanted to get a job. So I negotiated keeping on my voluntary placement job at a private therapy centre. I felt lucky to be able to do this as many of my peers could not do the same unless they wanted to work unpaid. I was paying a standard room rent for a block of hours and there was pressure to find my own clients. I did find that, even though I had numerous leaflets up in health-food shops, cafes and newsagents, I only ever seemed to get clients who were referred to me by someone else at the centre. Because they advertised themselves through magazines and Yellow Pages, maybe this communicated greater credibility then my leaflets could achieve.

Clive

After eight months of minimal income, I managed to get a regular part-time job from a friend of a friend. It made me aware that you don't find work by sitting down and waiting. Furthermore, I found it pointless labouring over application forms for newspaper-advertised positions because of the sheer number of better qualified and experienced counsellors who were already out there.

My advice to anyone entering training, or finishing it, is to assertively seek out work. Speak to people, meet them, tell them what you do and eventually, through your commitment and motivation, something will turn up. But you have to be very 'brass necked' and hugely enthusiastic.

Clare-Ann

I'm now in independent private practice, facilitate a small group for female survivors of childhood sexual abuse and work with an autistic child. I have led several experiential workshops and intend to develop this work. I have applied to an agency to lecture in adult colleges. Also I will be starting a counselling supervisor's course in October this year. I am awaiting the outcome of my BAC Accreditation application.

Focusing on some strands of my experience after I qualified, it is clear to me I had an extremely distressing time. Within the period of the first fifteen months, along-side voluntary counselling work, I made twenty applications — including job-search letters — for a part-time counselling job. I attended four interviews with genuine motivation, high enthusiasm and no luck! During that time, my needs and convictions were put to the severe test as I started to realise that I was not to find a job unless I somehow adopted an attitude of submissiveness to the inflexibility of rigid structures and shoestring budgets. Despite the pressures, the benefits were great in that I grew to know my needs as a practitioner in a more complete way and found the courage to respect them. For example, I was not prepared to offer a six-session counselling contract or see one client straight after the other or use a 'bits of person-centred' approach. Of course, my level of experience (not yet to BAC Accreditation) didn't help, notably on one sadly missed occasion too.

Ricki

Last but not least, six months ago, after thoughtful consideration and careful planning, I took up the challenge to set up as an individual counsellor. However slowly it is going, I am finding it most rewarding and challenging.

Tony
Latterly I was fortunate to be able to set up a counselling service for the staff of the Education Department of a Local Authority. This service was disbanded during the period of local government reorganisation. There remains an abiding sense that the risks were worth taking, the financial costs were high, my personal learning was significant and although I'm now working freelance and having to learn a new way of working, I would do it again. It was the right step at the time and further validated the process of growth and development which I've been committed to through a person-centred approach.

At present I have just taken up a research post at a local university in the area of stress management. So I am not counselling privately at the moment but ,once I know the impact this research job has on my time, I aim to start counselling again soon.
Isobel

Dorothy
It is now three and a half years since my Diploma ended. My private practice has been in operation for five years and it is growing and developing very quickly. Once the Diploma finished, I took nearly two years off from studying but then began an MSc in Supervision and Training. At present I am halfway through the second and final year, again facing the task of writing another dissertation but this time 15,000 words! I work as a school counsellor for one and a half days a week, spend one day a week at the College for my MSc and for the remaining two and a half days I see private clients at home.

It has taken me several years to settle into my work as a counsellor. In some ways I find this is as much to do with me finding my own style and approach which fits with who I am and how I want to practice. If jobs had come along quicker I'm not sure if I would have been ready for them.
Sharon

Lara
I have worked in student counselling at a college for about five years now. It has been a tremendously rewarding experience. For some reason, people who are not familiar with this environment think that student counselling is an 'easy' context in which to work. I find this as challenging as I'd imagine any other to be.

For about a year and a half after my training course, I continued to work in a voluntary capacity at a Gay Men's Health Centre, as a counsellor. They couldn't really afford to pay me but did cover my supervision costs and paid travel expenses. I had hoped this job would give me the work experience which could launch me into a decently paid counselling job. I got disillusioned and went back to nursing supply. I do not counsel anymore but I am a member of a couple of counselling associations and so keep in touch with what's going on. Maybe I'll get back into it one day?
Todd

Rathy
I have several counselling jobs. For two days I work at a GP practice, for two more I work at a 'Well-Woman' Centre and for a Friday and Saturday morning I work privately out of some offices I rent from a friend in town. All give me a different experience of what counselling is about.I don't favour one context more than another.

Tracey

This question prompt has been quite useful for me. 'Where are you now?' I suppose it makes me reflect on where I am physically with my work but more importantly whether this is right for me and why do we counsel. I work as a counsellor in primary care and do feel well supported by the line manager and my supervisor. But I often get days when I come back and I say to myself 'why do we do this?' I don't think it's about me not being able to handle client issues, neither is it about getting too involved with the client issues. I just think it is that I don't think we can be human if this sort of work doesn't have this affect on us. This work does drain me but even though I'm feeling a bit antipathetic about this, I'm not sure I can identify anything which can offer me the highs and satisfactions I get out of counselling.

Madeleine

I have come out of my counselling training with a very clear message about what I don't want to do. I don't want to be a counsellor. I managed to get my Diploma and did work as a counsellor privately for about six months thereafter. But I went back into my work with Community Service Volunteers as a Centre Director. The course has enabled me to be a better manager and also work with my teams more effectively. I actively encourage and promote more team development work and pay for every member to attend a counselling skills course.

points to ponder

• Before you begin further training, how can you see a career path ahead of you? People change during training so it may be difficult to plan but it may be worth keeping an eye on future developments and opportunities.

• Many people dislike the concept of 'networking' but if you look at this as a way to meet and learn through other people (counsellors/employers), you may find this becomes a valuable way to hear about job opportunities. Networking is not about *using* people — quite the opposite — it is about seeking opportunities from others under the proviso that you'd be willing to help them out similarly. A key consideration is that networking doesn't necessarily provide immediate results. It is about keeping in touch with a range of people who may be able to provide leads for you in the future. Whilst keeping in touch, you are doing two things. Firstly, you are reminding them that you exist and can update them on your services. Secondly, you can ask whether you can help them. It may take many months of this contact time before anything comes of it.

• If you plan to set up in private practice it might be useful to consider several points:
  a) How can you best promote yourself — word of mouth, leaflet drop, posters in well-chosen locations, advertisements in local press or trade journals, asking for referrals from different bodies or agencies, networking, promotional lunch-time workshops?

b) If you plan to work from home, are you happy to give out your phone number? Consider buying an answer machine so you can screen calls, if need be. Some telephone operators offer an 'individualised' number and ringing tone, so you can give out this phone number, aware that a particular ringing tone will indicate that a counselling-related call is coming through. Does your phone have a 'ringer-control' button which can be switched off during sessions? How will you choose to answer a phone call, not knowing whether it may be a friend or a distressed potential client?

c) Privacy, safety and comfort for you and your clients. Is the room quiet, warm, free from disruptions and furnished appropriately with suitable seating?

d) Professional liability insurance, who and what is covered? Do you need Public Liability Insurance? If you are working from home what cover is provided by your household insurance policies or are there certain exemptions?

e) Costs and payment procedures. Do you request payment after each session or would you invoice after/before? Will you operate a sliding scale based on ability to pay and, if so, can you realistically afford to do this (or not do this!)

f) If you are later offered a salaried position which interests you, what commitment will you have to any current private clients? How much notice would you give them that your circumstances are changing?

g) How will you manage your finances? Counsellors are more often paid in cash, offering temptations not to declare this to the relevant authorities. You would be advised to enlist the services of an accountant . . . and to declare all your income!

- Meet with people from different organisations (public and private sector, voluntary, educational, health) to find out if they have any counselling-related support for their employees. If they do, apply to that provider for work, if they don't, consider how you could find out their needs and ways you could help them out.

It is not a good idea to try to organise your career from the 'outside' of the profession. Do join at least one professional body or national organisation such as, BAPCA, the Association for Humanistic Psychology Practitioners (AHPP), Independent Practitioners Network (IPN), BAC, COSCA, or PCT Scotland. You will make important contacts, get to know of meetings in your area, find out about jobs and generally keep up-to-date with developments which will improve your employability.

All contact details for these organisations can be found in Appendix 3.

person-centred
counselling
training

25
one thing I wish I'd known before I started . . .

This final chapter brings us back to the beginning. It summarises why this book was compiled. We (Rick and Laura) followed different routes into counselling training and found this exhilarating, exciting, excruciating and entertaining. However, we felt that we could have been better prepared for what lay ahead. In consulting with many past, present and aspiring trainees, the same comment was often raised. It was more than just finding out how a particular course was run or the content of the curriculum. It was about *the experience*. Counselling training is an immensely personal affair and it is this angle which in retrospect would have been really valued and appreciated.

This book exists to give readers an idea about what training was like for some people. It is their personal (and sometimes intimate) account of *their* experience and should be best used to set the scene, to provide a flavour, offer an insight, not create unreasonable expectations or establish a *fait accompli*.

There are some 13 case-study comments to follow in this chapter. All respondents to the project wanted to make a comment on this topic, but for reasons of space — and to avoid repetition — it was necessary to make a random selection. The result represents a good cross-section of the views of the contributors.

In this section we have not highlighted specific issues raised from the case-studies — we thought it best that you read read them uninhibited. However, as a precursor, the editors will each share their 'one thing they wish they'd known'.

Laura would have liked to have understood better the *pace* of full-time training. At times, the commitment to experiential work and academic work left her reeling. She sometimes felt pressured and caught between how to best apply her time and energy to the course and how to meet her immediate personal needs within these commitments.

Rick jumped into a Diploma course, *thinking* he was ready and prepared. However, it was one thing to talk about it and quite another to experience it. He was quite unprepared for the depth of personal development work involved for him personally. Although this was necessary in order to best take on board the skills, values and qualities of learning to be a proficient counsellor, he wishes he'd had some sort of insight into the degree of change that was possible *and* that this might change his life. In short, he wished that someone had explained how personal development work is sometimes like jumping in at the deep end without knowing how deep the water is! The question is, could anyone have explained that to him?

Sophie   I wish I had known that it is very difficult to earn money as a counsellor. Having worked in private practice for about two years I have found it very precarious. People cancel at the last minute. They find it hard to find the money for the fees. It is very difficult to work solely as a counsellor, in my opinion, unless you are supported by an institution or company. It is very expensive work and although people say that there is a crying need for counsellors, no one wants to pay for them! You have to fund your own supervision. There is no clear professional career structure. It is a very Cinderella-like profession in the voluntary sector.

There is nothing I wish I'd known. I feel I had a good idea that I was going to feel   **Natalie**
challenged and extended, that I would change. The course itself was an adventure and a learning process which overall was a very positive experience, although sometimes very hard.

Having said all this, I feel that students were not aware of the self-understanding and self-searching required on a course of this nature, although by the end we had all changed in some way (positively). Part of me also feels that 40 hours of personal counselling is not enough for a Diploma course, especially when many students had never received counselling before the course.

Carla   In hindsight I wish I'd known two things — firstly, that I might meet my worst imaginable ethical dilemma and, secondly, how physically and emotionally draining it really is.

I wish I had a fuller understanding of what *self-awareness* and *self-development*   **Petula**
meant and what it takes to get there in terms of emotional energy.

Ruth   It would have been interesting to know how much of yourself is revealed on training courses.

I wish I'd appreciated how much time and emotional energy the course would   **Sandy**
require.

Maggie   I would like to have considered the possibility that I may fail. I knew I could not know this until I was on the course but perhaps it would have made me consider a different therapeutic approach. My money wasn't wasted but maybe it could have been put to better use.

Perhaps I would have liked to be aware how much it was going to change me, i.e.   **Ella**
the amount of personal development and personal counselling I was going to undertake.

Sheila   I would like to have known that I was not going to get a 'purely' person-centred experience. I find it interesting to write that soon after I finished training I decided to give myself a gift — for all my hard work and accomplishments — which was a person-centred residential weekend.

I found just completing the written work for this qualification excruciating because   *Lauren*
I did not know how to write essays and how to ascertain exactly what was wanted.
It would have been far better if I had known how to do this *before* starting the course.

Ricki   I wish I'd known more about the motivation and intentions of the trainers and
what brought them into counselling. All too often, trainers can remain distant and
mystical figures with no abusive past. But this is simply not true. Trainers have
investments in power on counselling courses. And if their training helps less and
harms more they should not be there. Other points or issues might include hidden
agendas and also the potential for collusion, and the subsequent dynamics, between
students and staff.

I would have liked to have known what the word *process* meant. We were put in   *Laurel*
groups and told to report on the *process*. After quite some time, the penny dropped
but did it need this wait?

Ronald   I wish I'd known about 'after-effects'; how dramatic and traumatic some personal
insights and awareness could be — unpicked by peers, tutors, workshops and
lectures. Then I could have communicated this to my partner, family and friends.
After all this, it seems a monumental 'process' to go through to then find out there
are practically no jobs around. This was soul-destroying and makes me wonder
whether this degree of development is worth it with little chance of 'using it'. This
book that I'm contributing to sounds like it could have given me the insight and
warnings in advance and prepared me in a no-holds-barred sort of way.

• What further questions do you have about training? Can you find the answers
   from people you know, local counsellors, training institutions, former
   trainees or the British Association for Counselling?

points to ponder

• Are you emotionally ready to take on the tough challenge of counselling
   training? Do not worry if the answer for you is 'No', not everyone is.

• If you have read this book chapter by chapter, you should have gained a
   better insight into the experience of counselling training. Now make a careful
   note of questions which have risen for you or to record concerns you have.
   Make sure you raise these with the appropriate people — relatives, tutors
   or whoever — entering into training is a big decision

• Hopefully, having read this book, you will be better prepared to decide whether
   counselling training is for you. Do not be overawed by tutors or the
   application procedure. In a truly person-centred course, you should feel
   listened to and respected, and you will be expected to be honest in your
   responses.

• Good luck.

The following represents a range of possible costs incurred during training and exclude any further living costs incurred by studying away from home, e.g. accommodation/food etc.

Appendix 1

funding issues: a checklist of course costs

	£	
Interview fee	____	
Enrolment fee	____	
Tuition/registration/matriculation fees	____	per term/year
Text books — pre-course reading list	____	
— course reading list	____	
Stationary incl. assignment binders etc	____	
Photocopying	____	
Professional Associations — subscription fees	____	
Supervision costs	____	per term/year
Personal Counselling costs	____	per term/year
Personal/Professional Indemnity Insurance	____	per year
Residential fees for special weekends/units/modules	____	
Training aids e.g. tape recorder, blank tapes etc	____	
Travel costs	____	per term/year
Graduation fee	____	
Extra workshops, guest speakers	____	
Other add-on courses	____	

Total   ____

Some courses make a charge for interviewing you for your place on the course.

Some charge separately for course tuition, registration for examinations and again to pay for your certificate or diploma.

Some courses have compulsory 'extra' elements, such as residential units or weekends, for which you may have to pay separately.

Check all this before you enrol, preferably during the interview.

**experi-
ences
of**

person-centred
counselling
training

Appendix
2

recom-
mended
further
reading

The Person-Centred Approach — introductory texts for beginners
Mearns, D. and Thorne, D. (1999) *Person-Centred Counselling in Action —
     Second Edition.* London: Sage Publications.
Merry, T. (1995) *Invitation to Person-Centred Psychology.* London: Whurr.
Merry, T. (1999) *Leraning and Being in Person-Centred Counselling.* Ross-
     on-Wye: PCCS Books.

The Person-Centred Approach — more advanced
Axline, V. (1990) *Dibs: In Search of Self.* Harmondsworth: Pelican
Rogers, C. (1961) *On Becoming a Person.* Boston: Houghton Mifflin.
Rogers, C.R. and Stevens, B. (1994) *Person to Person: The Problem of Being
     Human.* London: Souvenir Press.
Thorne, B. J. (1992) *Carl Rogers.* London: Sage.

General introductory texts
Frankland, A. and Sanders, P. (1995) *Next Steps in Counselling.* Ross-on-Wye:
     PCCS Books.
Sanders, P. (1998) (Second Edition) *First steps in Counselling.* Ross on Wye:
     PCCS Books.

Special areas
Bond, T. (1993) *Standards and Ethics for Counselling in Action.* London:
     Sage Publications.
Davies, D. and McNeal, C. (1996) *Pink Therapy.* Buckingham: Open University
     Press.
Lago, C. with Thompson, L. (1996) *Race, Culture and Counselling.*
     Buckingham: Open University Press.
Thorne, B. (1991) *Person-Centred Counselling: Therapeutic and Spiritual
     Dimensions.* London: Whurr.

To find out about other approaches
Dryden, W. (1996) *Handbook of Individual Therapy.* London: Sage
     Publications.

Assessment and assignments
MacMillan, M. and Clark, D. (1998) *Learning and Writing in Counselling.*
     London: Sage Publications.
Sanders, P. (1998) (Second Edition) *Step in to Study Counselling.* Ross-on-
     Wye: PCCS Books.

Person-Centred

British Association for the Person-Centred Approach (BAPCA):
For membership details, and other information write to BM BAPCA, London, WC1N 3XX, or telephone 01989 770 948. You can also email: info@bapca.org.uk
Website: www.bapca.org.uk

Person-Centred Therapy Scotland (PCTS):
For all information write to 40 Kelvingrove St, Glasgow, G3 7RZ, or telephone 0141 332 6888.

General

British Association for Counselling (BAC):
For membership and other details, write to: BAC, 1, Regent Place, Rugby, Warwickshire CV21 2PJ, or telephone 01788 550899. You can also email BAC at bac@bac.co.uk
Website: www.counselling.co.uk

Confederation of Scottish Counselling Agencies (COSCA):
For membership and other details contact 18 Viewfield St, Stirling, SK8 1UA Scotland, or telephone 01786 475 140.
Website: cosca.org.uk

Association of Humanistic Psychology Practitioners (AHPP):
For membership and other details, write to BCM AHPP, London WC1N 3XX, or telephone 0345 660 326. You can also email: ahp@saqnet.co.uk.

Independent Practitioners Network (IPN):
326 Burley Rd, Leeds, LS4 2NZ or telephone 0113 275 5984. You can also email: 100532.2353@compuserve.com.
Website: www.psyctc.org/mirrors/non-main/ipn

First Steps in Counselling 2nd edition
A Students' Companion for Basic Introductory Courses

Pete Sanders
1996 ISBN 1 898059 14 4 200x200 pp138+vi £11.00

This bestselling book is used as the standard course text on hundreds of basic introduction to counselling courses in colleges and independent training institutes throughout the UK. Now in its second edition it comprehensively covers the theory, skills and contextual issues of counselling in the 1990s for all those wanting an introduction to counselling. Each year some 5000 volunteers, social workers, carers, teachers, nurses, community workers, managers, beginning counsellors and their trainers use *First Steps in Counselling* as their starting point for learning.

'This is the second edition of a remarkable book. Its title suggests that it is for beginners only but this is far too modest a claim. . .

The reader is swept into companionship with a trainer and practitioner who knows his subject from top to bottom and who is keenly alert to the whole range of tensions that arise as counselling 'comes of age' in our society. Pete makes no apology for confronting his beginners with some of the harsh realities of what it means to be a counsellor as the twentieth century draws to a close.

At no point, however, does he assume an authoritarian or prescriptive stance. He imparts information — some of it complex and detailed — with lightness of touch . . .

For beginners and their tutors this book will be a resource without price but for the seasoned practitioner, too, it offers much more than an elegant revision course.'
         Professor Brian Thorne

'. . . highly accessible with good use of text, diagrams, discussion points and exercises. Sanders' writing style and his creative and appropriate use of poems and popular song lyrics is engaging and adds to the accessible quality and tone of this impressive series*. With suggestions on reading, personal exploration and development, the books parallel — and truly accompany — the learning process.'
         Keith Tudor *Person Centred Practice, Vol.5 No.1*

The new introduction to PERSON-CENTRED counselling from its origins to current developments in theory and practice

LEARNING AND BEING IN PERSON-CENTRED COUNSELLING
A TEXTBOOK FOR DISCOVERING THEORY AND DEVELOPING PRACTICE

Tony Merry *with additional material by Bob Lusty*
ISBN 1 898059 24 1   156x234 pp approx 180+iv

THIS BOOK IS a complete rewrite and extended version of the successful *What is Person-Centred Therapy* by Tony Merry and Bob Lusty previously published by the Gale Centre. At almost twice the size of the original, it contains new, up-to-date material and offers in-depth discussion of all aspects of person-centred counselling in theory and practice.

The coverage of the topics is innovative, comprehensive and thorough. Tony Merry is renowned for his straightforward and accessible writing style, making *Learning and Being in Person-Centred Counselling* suitable for a wide variety of readers.

Augmenting the clear presentation, the book is brought to life by many suggestions for exploring and developing person-centred values, qualities, attitudes and skills.

LEARNING AND BEING IN PERSON-CENTRED COUNSELLING is recommended for:
- certificate and diploma in counselling trainees and tutors;
- undergraduate psychology students and lecturers;
- nurses and social workers in training;
- those on vocational and professional helping professions-related courses;
- trainees on integrative, cognitive or psychodynamic courses;
- anyone seeking input on contemporary person-centred theory and practice.

CHAPTERS INCLUDE
- Human nature, actualisation and the development of the person;
- A theory of counselling;
- Developing person-centred values, skills, qualities and attitudes;
- Training issues: client work and personal development;
- Supervision;
- Working and being in groups;
- Resources;

TONY MERRY teaches at the University of East London on postgraduate and undergraduate courses in counselling and counselling psychology. He is author of several books and articles on counselling. He co-founded the British Association for the Person-Centred Approach in 1989 and is currently editor of *Person-Centred Practice* and the *Universities Psychotherapy Association Review.* He has contributed to workshops and other person-centred events in Europe, including several with Carl Rogers in England, Ireland and Hungary in the 1980s.

Bob Lusty worked closely with Tony Merry at the University of East London for over 20 years. He is now in private practice as a counsellor and supervisor.